2-18-84

4

a-10-12-78
B-11-3-78
C-11-5-78
3:40 PM

SIXTY YEARS OF VAMPS AND CAMPS

SIXTY YEARS OF VAMPS AND CAMPS

Visual Nostalgia of the Silver Screen

by Richard Hudson

with an introduction by Martha Raye

DRAKE PUBLISHERS INC.   NEW YORK

Published in 1973 by
Drake Publishers Inc.
381 Park Avenue South
New York, New York 10016

© Richard M. Hudson, 1973

Library of Congress Cataloging in Publication Data

Hudson, Richard M.
   Sixty years of vamps and camps.

   1. Moving-pictures—Pictorial works.   I. Title.
PN1993.5.A1H78   791.43'0292'2   73-5569
ISBN 0-87749-523-8

Printed in the United States of America

Book designed by Spencer Drate and Jill Taffet of Morninglight Productions

DEDICATION

For Mom, who should'da been in pictures, and for Alice and Robert Tardif. Alice could have been big but daddy wouldn't hear of it. He needed help behind the notions counter. For George Wilbern who was in pictures but prefers to show them on three screens at a time at his strange bar in San Francisco. Lastly to Robert Opel who had nothing to do with pictures. He used to be a teacher, but he's all right now.

TABLE OF CONTENTS

1   Off To Camp

2   Ladies Who Were Born To Be Bad

3   The Incredible Costumes

4   The Sex Gods And Goddesses

5   The Horror Films
(that made you shake
from either fear or laughter)

6   The Fabulous Musicals

7   Seven Movie Queens

"I appeared on television in 1971 in a series called "Bugaloos," playing a rock witch who lives in a noisy jukebox. With all the wild makeup for that role, including that nose, I got a kick out of children recognizing me in street clothes, saying: "there goes Benita Bizarre."

INTRODUCTION BY MARTHA RAYE

What is camp? I always thought camp was a place to go. Army camp, for instance. I made a few trips there!

In the late 1930's I went to camp with such wonderful personalities as Bob Burns, Jack Benny, George Burns and Gracie Allen, and, of course, Bob Hope. But in those days, it wasn't called "camp." We realized that the films we were making were "fun" pictures, but we didn't really realize that this relatively new art form would live on for so many years through television and "movie buff" theatres.

I'm sure you will enjoy, as I have, the many photographs in this book, which are not only cinema history, but a good explanation of American styles and tastes of our time. So, from Theda Bara to Raquel Welch, let's go OFF TO CAMP.

ACKNOWLEDGEMENTS

The photographs in this book
were made for publicity purposes
at the following studios:

Allied Artists
American International
Cinema Center Films
Columbia Pictures Corporation
Walt Disney Productions
Embassy Pictures Corporation
Samuel Goldwyn Productions
Magna Pictures Distributing Corp.
Metro-Goldwyn-Mayer Studios
Paramount Pictures Corporation
Republic Productions, Inc.
RKO Radio Pictures, Inc.
Hal Roach Favorite Films Corp.
Selznick International Productions
Seven Arts Associated Corporation
20th Century Fox
United Artists Corporation
Universal International
Warner Brothers Pictures, Inc.

For informative assistance or
the loan of rare photographs,
the author is grateful to:

Robert Wade Chatterton

The Academy of Motion Picture
Arts and Sciences Library,
Robert Cushman

Timothy Custer
Ray Gain
A. Wymer Gard
James Hudman
Mark Johnson
Dale E. Kuntz
Robert Osborne
James Robert Parish
Gene Ringgold

And very special thanks to:

Miss Martha Raye
DeWitt Bodeen
Myron Braum
Albert Lord
Gunnard Nelson
Robert Opel

1

OFF TO CAMP

Mary Pickford, 1917.

Shirley Temple
in BABY TAKE A BOW, 1934.

Sonja Henie
in MY LUCKY STAR, 1938.

Bette Davis
in WHAT EVER HAPPENED
TO BABY JANE?, 1962.

The NEW MOVIE MAGAZINE

AUGUST 1931

10¢ IN U.S. 15 CENTS IN CANADA

THE LARGEST CIRCULATION OF ANY SCREEN MAGAZINE IN THE WORLD

HELEN TWELVETREES

COULD YOU be a MOVIE STAR?

Turn to Page 33 and Find Out

WILL HAYS Tells the INSIDE STORY

The lady with the weird name, Helen Twelvetrees, "made" the cover of "The NEW Movie Magazine" for August, 1931.

Bring on the Cleo's. Theda Bara as CLEOPATRA (with Fritz Leiber), 1917.

Henry Wilcoxon and Claudette Colbert in CLEOPATRA, 1934.

Joan Davis as Cleopatra in SHOW BUSINESS, 1943.

Raymond Burr and Rhonda Fleming in SERPENT OF THE NILE, 1952.

Stewart Granger and Vivien Leigh in CAESAR AND CLEOPATRA, 1946.

Elizabeth Taylor as CLEOPATRA, 1963.

Shirley MacLaine and Dick Van Dyke in a take-off of the silent screen in WHAT A WAY TO GO!, 1964.

Clifton Webb and Ginger Rogers as silent screen lovers in DREAM BOAT, 1952.

"Will I end up in the closet like all the others?" says silent screen vamp Gloria Swanson in BLUEBEARD'S EIGHTH WIFE, 1923.

The great silent screen lover, Rudolph Valentino, posed casually on the set of MONSIEUR BEAUCAIRE, 1924.

Groucho Marx, Margaret Dumont and Sig Rumann in A NIGHT AT THE OPERA, 1935.

The Marx Brothers' real father and Harpo, Groucho, Chico, and Zeppo pose for a publicity shot for DUCK SOUP, 1933.

The silent screen's Ben Turpin crossed eyes weren't fake, but his moustache sure was.

Charlie Chaplin's "most famous portrait sitting."

"Everyone's Gone To The Moon," and so have Laurel and Hardy with a little help from the studio's art department in this publicity photo.

Stan Laurel and Oliver Hardy in BABES IN TOYLAND, 1934.

Laurel and Hardy help Jean Harlow (who was an extra player then) out of her taxi, and Laurel is the only one who knows that Miss Harlow's dress is caught in the door. DOUBLE WHOOPEE, 1929.

Buddy Rogers and Richard Arlen were "bosom buddies" in WINGS, 1927.

Louise Fazenda and Thelma Todd in VAMPING VENUS, 1928.

Clark Gable and Jean Harlow in RED DUST, 1932.
Memorable line —Jean, cleaning her bird cage, suddenly stops, looks at the bird, and says: "What they been feedin' ya, cement?"

12 STAR TRIUMPH!

Now Comes the Year's Most Celebrated Hit!

★ MARIE DRESSLER
★ JOHN BARRYMORE
★ WALLACE BEERY
★ JEAN HARLOW
★ LIONEL BARRYMORE
★ LEE TRACY
★ EDMUND LOWE
★ BILLIE BURKE
★ MADGE EVANS ★ KAREN MORLEY
★ JEAN HERSHOLT ★ PHILLIPS HOLMES

DINNER at 8

"DINNER AT 8" flames with drama...the fallen matinee idol...the millionaire's frivolous wife...the amorous doctor of the idle rich...stolen hours of romance...each thrilling episode played by a great STAR! No wonder it was Broadway's advanced-price film sensation for three months. It is YOURS with a thousand thrills NOW!

Screen play by Frances Marion and Herman J. Mankiewicz. From the Sam H. Harris stage play by GEORGE S. KAUFMAN & EDNA FERBER. Produced by David O. Selznick. Directed by George Cukor.

METRO·GOLDWYN·MAYER

1933

Although he was asked not to, Marie Dressler's dog has just done his thing in the hotel corridor. DINNER AT EIGHT, 1933.

Gloria Swanson (left) claims she did not get her start as a bathing beauty in early Mack Sennett comedies, but this photo proves she was one of the girls.

Norma Shearer as a bathing beauty, 1923.

Greta Garbo (left) was a bathing beauty in her first film, PETER THE TRAMP, 1922.

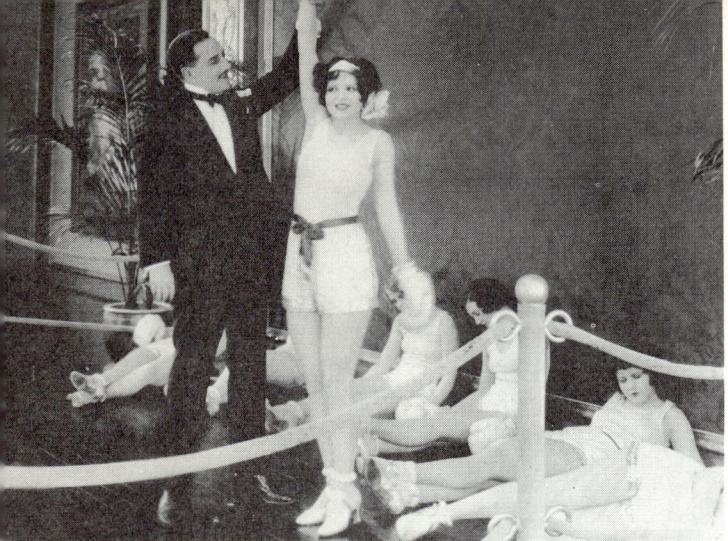

Long before lady wrestlers were on television we got to see Clara Bow knock 'em all out in ROUGH HOUSE ROSIE, 1927.

Helen Kane (the boop boop-a-doop girl) and Stuart Erwin in SWEETIE, 1929.

William Powell, Richard "Skeets" Gallagher, and Helen Kane in POINTED HEELS, 1929.

Could things be as bad as their expressions lead us to believe? Regis Toomey and Clara Bow in KICK IN, 1931.

Marie Dressler and Polly Moran have just read about the stock market crash in CAUGHT SHORT, 1930.

Marie Dressler as Venus in THE HOLLYWOOD REVUE OF 1929.

Beatrice Lillie in THOROUGHLY MODERN MILLIE, 1967.

Greer Garson is getting her kicks in MRS. PARKINGTON, 1944.

Roland Young and Billie Burke in TOPPER, 1937.

Eddie "Rochester" Anderson, Roland Young, and Billie Burke in TOPPER RETURNS, 1941.

Billie Burke, Alex D'Arcy, and Roland Young in TOPPER TAKES A TRIP, 1938.

Hattie McDaniel, Jean Parker, and Billie Burke in ZENOBIA, 1939.

Elsa Lanchester, Jeanette MacDonald, and Frank Morgan in NAUGHTY MARIETTA, 1935.

In LADIES IN RETIREMENT, 1941, Ida Lupino wonders what her demented sisters, Edith Barrett and Elsa Lanchester will do next. The sisters spend their time cleaning up the seashore. This was prior to the present concern with ecology and oil slicks.

Elsa Lanchester, Kim Novak, and Jack Lemmon were all witches in BELL, BOOK, and CANDLE, 1958.

Fanny Brice and William Frawley in ZIEGFELD FOLLIES, 1946.

Martha Raye put this beauty facial on to become gorgeous for her evening's date, but it hardened and would not com off! GIVE ME A SAILOR, 1938.

Another beauty facial is for Gloria Swanson, getting her ready for her "comeback" in SUNSET BOULEVARD, 1950.

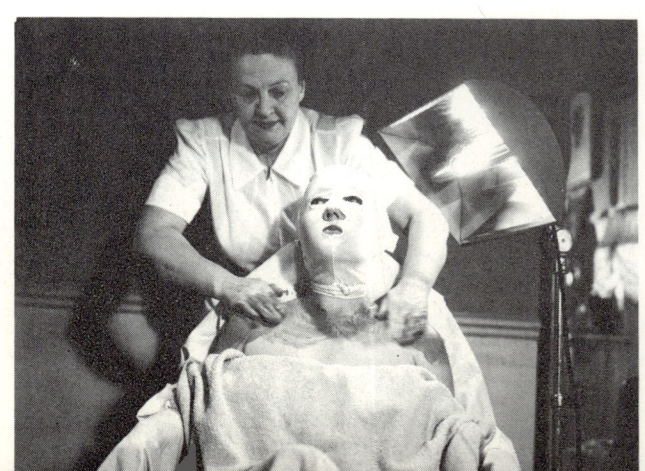

␣e Jergens and Cornel Wilde in A ␣USAND AND ONE NIGHTS, 1945.

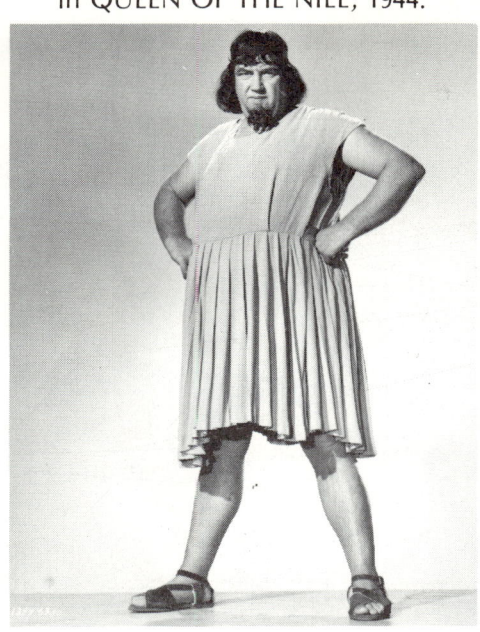

Andy Devine didn't play the title role in QUEEN OF THE NILE, 1944.

The QUEEN OF THE NILE was none other than Maria Montez.

Turhan Bey and Gloria Grahame in PRISONERS OF THE CASBAH, 1953.

Linda Ho, Vincent Price, and June Kim in CONFESSIONS OF AN OPIUM EATER, 1962.

Olivia DeHavilland in THAT LADY, 1955.

Bette Davis in THE ANNIVERSARY, 1968.

If a list of ten all-time, super camp films were made, THE WOMEN, 1939, would rank high. Here are Phyllis Povah, Paulette Goddard, Joan Crawford, Rosalind Russell, Mary Boland (seated), Norma Shearer, and Florence Nash (seated) in a feminine battle of wits all of which concerns men.

THE OPPOSITE SEX, 1956, was a remake of THE WOMEN and was as poor as most remakes are. Here are Joan Collins, Dolores Gray, Jeff Richards, Ann Sheridan, Ann Miller, Joan Blondell, and Agnes Moorehead.

ou may wonder if Norma Shearer found her other shoe fore she went to the alter in A LADY OF CHANCE, 1929.

Mary Boland in MELODY IN SPRING, 1934.

"I'll get you, my pretty, and your little dog too." argaret Hamilton as the wicked witch of the West in THE WIZARD OF OZ, 1939.

Margaret Hamilton as Mrs. Golightly in THE SUN COMES UP, 1949. She is about to teach Jeanette MacDonald the proper art of chewing tobacco.

You may not recognize the blonde, but it's Eleanor Powell (with Jack Benny) in THE BROADWAY MELODY OF 1936.

A slight scratch doesn't keep Hedy Lamarr
(an aging movie queen) from rubbing noses with young
and often shirtless George Nader
in THE FEMALE ANIMAL, 1958.

Jane Powell ducked out from her
girl-next-door roles to become Hedy's alcoholic daughter,
also in love with George Nader, in THE FEMALE ANIMAL.
Jan Sterling (right) added the necessary touches
to make this film a pretty good expression of "camp."

Hedy Lamarr as Joan of Arc in THE STORY OF MANKIND, 1957.

Miss Harlow and Alice Faye (pictured here) seemed to be in a look-alike contest for two or threee years in the 1930's.

While shaving eyebrows and painting on new ones was popular in the 1930's, a few stars went slightly overboard. JEAN HARLOW.

And not to be overlooked, Ida Lupino.

Lew Ayres and Alice Faye
in SHE LEARNED ABOUT SAILORS, 1934.

Carmen Miranda, Shelia Ryan, and Alice Faye
in THE GANG'S ALL HERE, 1943.

Gail Patrick, Norma Drury, Constance Collier,
Ginger Rogers, and Lucille Ball in STAGE DOOR, 1937.

Fred Astaire, Ginger Rogers, and in a bit part,
Lucille Ball. FOLLOW THE FLEET, 1936.

Lucille Ball and Harpo Marx in ROOM SERVICE, 1938.

Remember how young Lucy and Desi looked in their television series? This was taken over ten years prior to the series, from TOO MANY GIRLS, 1940, when they first met.

James Mason and Lucille Ball playing house in FOREVER, DARLING, 1956.

Red Skelton and Lucille Ball
in DU BARRY WAS A LADY, 1943.

A hairdo to end all hairdos—
this one has a bird cage with
a live bird in it.
Lucille Ball and Bob Hope
in FANCY PANTS, 1950.

Miss Ball and Vivian Vance
on Lucy's television show, 1964.

Long before she became the perfect wife on the screen,
Myrna Loy was type-cast as an Oriental.
Here is how she appeared in THE MASK OF FU MANCHU, 1932.

Myrna Loy and Monte Blue in ACROSS THE PACIFIC, 1926, the first of Miss Loy's native-type roles.

Primo Carnera, Myrna Loy, and Max B
in THE PRIZEFIGHTER AND THE LADY,

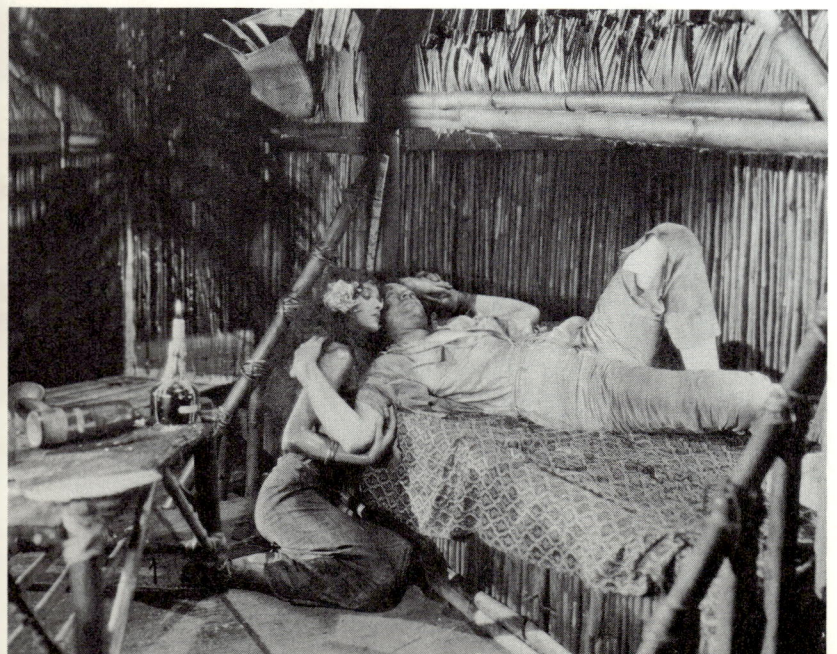

William Powell, Myrna Loy, Asta, and the fire hydrant in THE THIN MAN GOES HOME, 1944.

Cary Grant and Myrna Loy (as a judge) in THE BACHELOR AND THE BOBBY SOXER, 1947. The Bobby Soxer was none other than Shirley Temple.

First film of a popular series was THE THIN MAN, 1934, which began Myrna Loy's string of perfect-wife roles. Here are Miss Loy, Maureen O'Sullivan, William Powell, and the lovable, four-legged prankster, "Asta".

Myrna Loy, William Powell, and Sheldon Leonard (who may burn a hole in his pocket) in ANOTHER THIN MAN, 1939.

Rosalind Russell and Norma Shearer in THE WOMEN, 1939. Miss Russell is announcing the fact that her nails are "jungle red."

Ralph Bellamy, Cary Grant, and Rosalind Russell in HIS GIRL FRIDAY, 1940.

Rosalind Russell and Helen Vinson in LIVE, LOVE, AND LEARN, 1937.

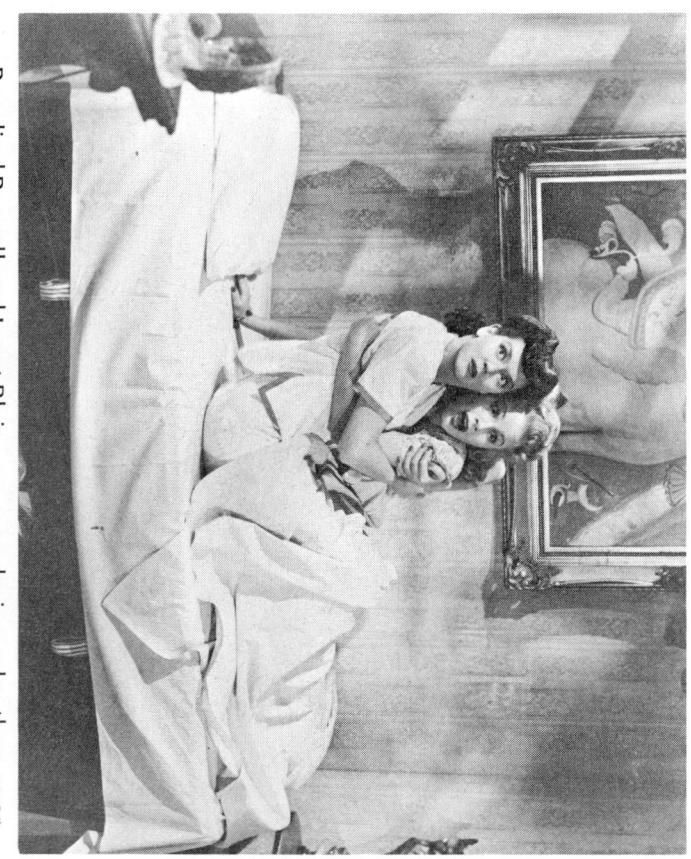

Rosalind Russell and Janet Blair are wondering why they ever left Ohio to go to the big city in MY SISTER EILEEN, 1942.

"Your Auntie Mame is hung," exclaims Rosalind Russell to her nephew while trying to get it together in AUNTIE MAME, 1958.

On the way to the PICNIC, 1956, Arthur O'Connell had coaxed Rosalind Russell to take one little teeny drink. She did.

"Life is a banquet, and most poor suckers are starving to death," says Rosalind Russell as AUNTIE MAME.

You'd probably never guess, but it's Jeanette MacDonald, before she had made a Hollywood film.
And here's Jeanette in a similar pose for her first film, THE LOVE PARADE, 1929.

Jeanette MacDonald, upon being introduced to Annabelle —ing, a member of her fan club, said: "I once made a picture —th your name in the title. If you ever get a chance to see it, —n't." ANNABELLE'S AFFAIRS, 1931.

William Austin, Richard "Skeets" Gallagher, James Hall, Kay Francis, Jeanette MacDonald, and Jack Oakie in LETS GO NATIVE, 1930.

LOVE ME TONIGHT, 1932, holds up today as one of the most delightful films of all-time. Here is the assembled cast: C. Aubrey Smith, Charlie Ruggles, Maurice Chevalier, Myrna Loy, Jeanette MacDonald, Charles Butterworth, and Elizabeth Patterson.

Charles Butterworth falls off this ladder while romancing Jeanette MacDonald, and when she asks if he is hurt, he replies: "No. I fell flat on my flute." LOVE ME TONIGHT, 1932.

Myrna Loy, Maurice Chevalier, and Jeanette MacDonald in LOVE ME TONIGHT. When Myrna Loy is asked if she could go for a doctor after Jeanette MacDonald has fainted she replies: "Oh yes! Send him right in."

Jeanette MacDonald in I MARRIED AN ANGEL, 1942.

If you were a big star at a big studio, you could have your choice of rounded wings or pointed wings.

Ethel Waters and Jeanette MacDonald in CAIRO, 1942. In this scene, when San Francisco is mentioned, Jeanette says: "I was in SAN FRANCISCO once, with Gable and Tracy, and the whole place fell apart."

Or you could have traded in your wings for a halo. Nelson Eddy and Jeanette MacDonald in I MARRIED AN ANGEL.

Ginger Rogers in a short called OFFICE BLUES, 1930, before she made her first feature film.

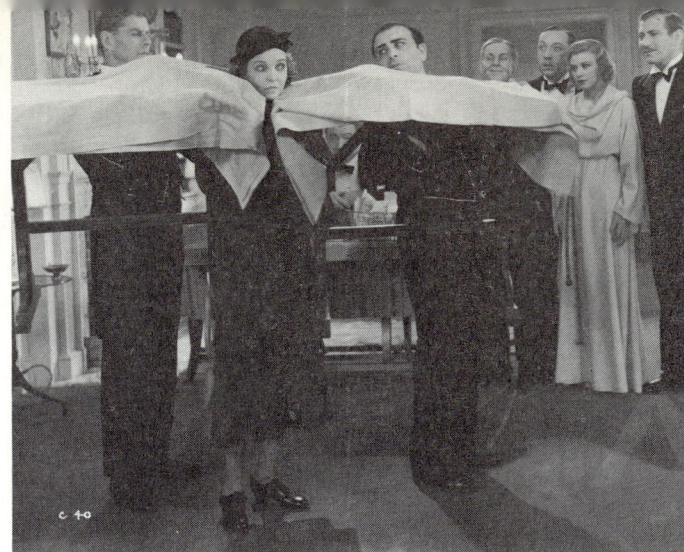
ZaSu Pitts, and (far right) Franklyn Pangborn, Ginger Rogers and Gregory Ratoff in PROFESSIONAL SWEETHEART,

Ginger Rogers caught her dress in this trunk in THE GAY DIVORCEE, 1934, and met Fred Astaire with the embarrassment of having her knees in full view.

Helen Broderick (left) gave great camp touches in all her film appearances, especially in a Ginger Rogers-Fred Astaire film. Here she is with Ginger in TOP HAT, 1935.

Eve Arden, Lucille Ball, Ann Miller (in background), and Ginger Rogers in STAGE DOOR, 1937.

Adolphe Menjou and Ginger Rogers in ROXIE HART, 1942.
The film was billed as the story of "a girl who could do no wrong,
but brother she tried." The publicity averred as to how it "was spiced with Ginger."

Ginger Rogers (with dark hair) and her real mother, Lelia Rogers,
in THE MAJOR AND THE MINOR, 1942.

Carole Landis, Betty Grable, and Charlotte Greenwood came to Miami to snag rich husbands in MOON OVER MIAMI, 1941.

Tom Mix on the left, but did you ever think Mickey Rooney was this small? MY PAL, THE KING, 1932.

This pose could mean just about anything. Kay Francis and Walter Huston in THE VIRTUOUS SIN,

Claudette Colbert and Clark Gable in IT HAPPENED ONE NIGHT, 1934.

Claudette Colbert had a lot to learn about laying eggs when she married Fred MacMurray in THE EGG AND I, 1946.

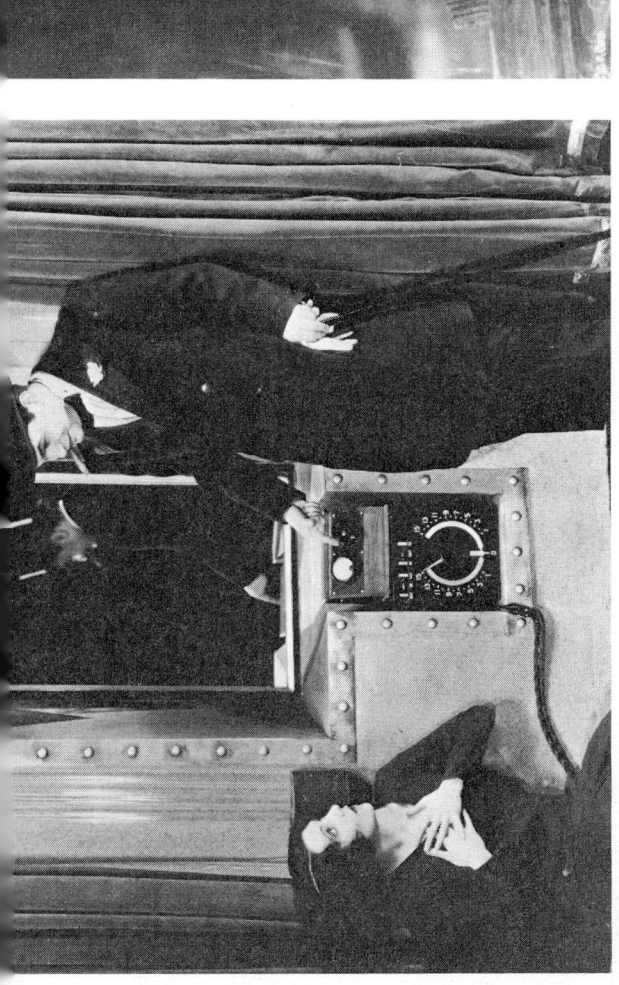

Claudette Colbert and Edward G. Robinson in THE HOLE IN THE WALL, 1929.

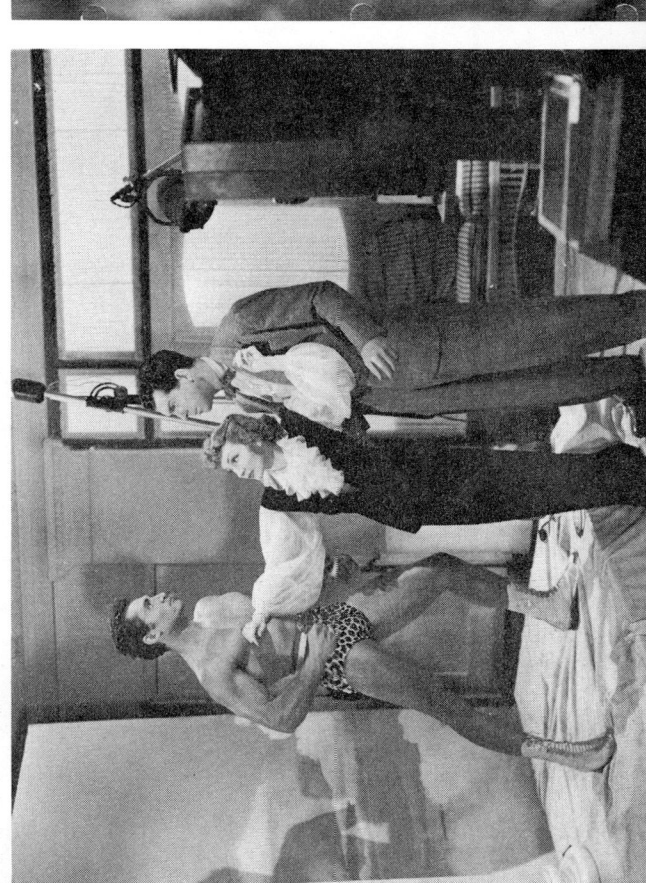

This photo may well describe the title of the film, NO TIME FOR LOVE, 1943, with Jerry D'Nuccio, Claudette Colbert, and Fred MacMurray.

Gary Cooper didn't always hold his cigarette like that,
and Marlene Dietrich doesn't seem too happy about sitting around
that particular day having to pose for publicity stills. MOROCCO, 1930.

Marlene Dietrich in TOUCH OF EVIL, 1958.

Rita Hayworth wasn't always a star. Here she is a publicity pose for CHARLIE CHAN IN EGYPT, 1935.

Larry Simms as "Baby Dumpling" and Rita Hayworth in BLONDIE ON A BUDGET, 1940.

Marilyn Monroe, Cary Grant, and Charles Coburn in MONKEY BUSINESS, 1952.

Ethel Merman, Dan Dailey, Mitzi Gaynor, Donald O'Connor, and Marilyn Monroe in THERE'S NO BUSINESS LIKE SHOW BUSINESS, 1954.

Kim Novak is the one who should be upset, at having to wear an outfit like that. Judy Holliday, Jack Lemmon, and Kim in PHFFFT, 1954.

Judy Holliday as Billie Dawn in BORN YESTERDAY, 1950.

Legend has it that Lana Turner was discovered itting on a soda-fountain stool. Maybe not, but she did sip a soda in her first feature film, THEY WON'T FORGET, 1937.

Jeff Chandler and Lana Turner in THE LADY TAKES A FLYER, 1958.

A swimming suit fashion show seemed to be the main plot of LOVE HAS MANY FACES, 1964, with Lana Turner and Hugh O'Brian.

Barbara Stanwyck and Rod LaRocque in THE LOCKED DOOR, 1929.

Waiting for the next dime are Sally Blane (Loretta Young's sister) and Barbara Stanwyck in TEN CENTS A DANCE, 1931.

Here's the mother with absolutely no taste in fashion and grooming and the daughter ashamed to be seen with her in public. Barbara Stanwyck and Anne Shirley in STELLA DALLAS, 1937.

ver take candy from a stranger. Walter McGrail and Barbara Stanwyck in NIGHT NURSE, 1931.

Miss Stanwyck never had trouble handling a gun, and this time the Western was even in 3-D! THE MOONLIGHTER, 1953.

Jane Russell and Bob Hope in THE PALEFACE, 1948.

Humphery Bogart and Rosemary Lane in THE RETURN OF DR. X, 19

This book could not be complete without Vera Hruba Ralston, (shown here with Forrest Tucker in JUBILEE TRAIL, 1954.) She married Herbert Yates, head boss of Republic Studios, and she appeared as a star exclusively in his pictures.

Victor Mature and Anne Bancroft in THE LAST FRONTIER, 19

"The Wampas Baby Stars of 1935" is actually what they were called. And here are six of the girls "most likely to succeed." (bottom, left to right): Gail Patrick, Gertrude Michael, Wendy Barrie, and (top): Katherine DeMille, Grace Bradley, and Ann Sheridan.

Rock Hudson and Barbara Rush in TAZA, SON OF COCHISE 1953.

Ann Sheridan, Ida Lupino, Richard Arlen, and Toby Wing in COME ON, MARINES, 1934.

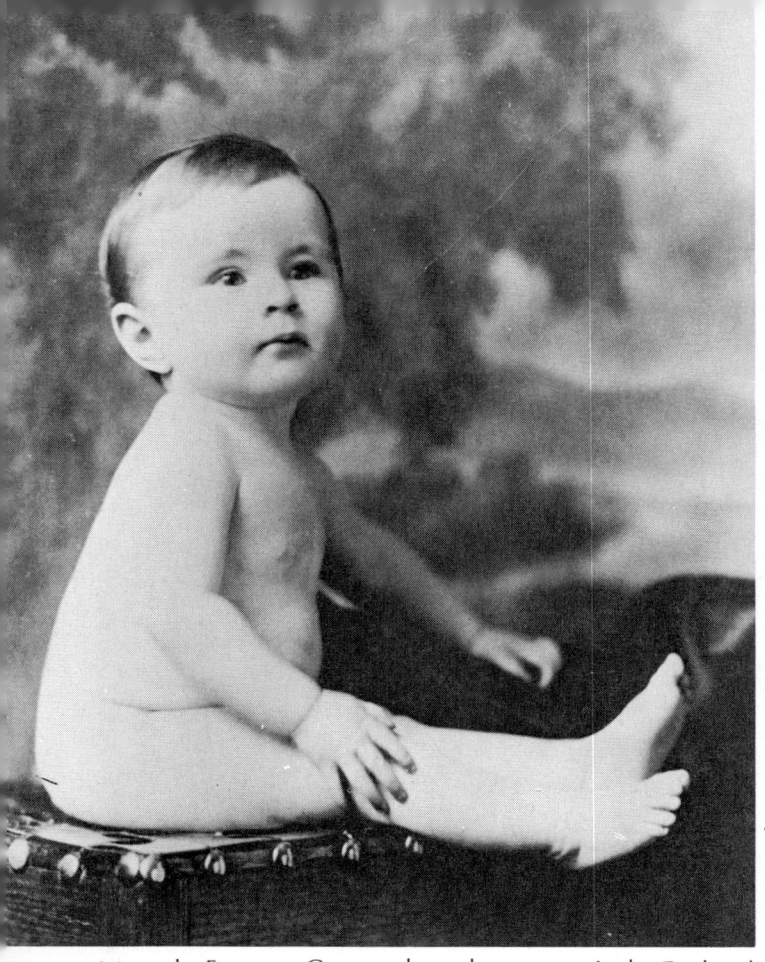

It's little Frances Gumm, later known as Judy Garland.

It's doubtful that this sleigh will go very far, it has no horse, poor Judy Garland had to sit under the hot studio lights, in Southern California yet, to pose for this!

And little Frances had two sisters, (Sue (left), and Gim known in vaudeville circuits as, precisely enough "The Gumm Sisters." Later in her career, Judy said of the act: "We were really......terrible."

Deanna Durbin and Judy Garland in EVERY SUNDAY, 1936, made shortly before either one of them had made a feature fi

Judy Garland in EVERYBODY SING, 1938.

Judy and Fanny Brice in the same film.

Jack Haley, Patsy Kelly, Stuart Erwin, Judy Garland, Johnny Downs, and Betty Grable in PIGSKIN PARADE, 1936.

Judy Garland in a costume test for THE WIZARD OF OZ, 1939. Notice two different Ruby slippers! This entire outfit was "shelved."

Here's a second try for Judy. But this wig and dre were not worn in the finished print, either.

And here's the final decision, which was a good one, considering that at a recent auction this dress sold for $1,000 and the ruby slippers went for $15,000. Judy is with Ray Bolger and Jack Haley.

Fay Bainter (right) has reservations about the hat that Judy Garland brought her, in PRESENTING LILY MARS, 1943.

When neighbors swiped all the steaks from the restaurant Judy Garland worked in, she went to retrieve the food like this. THE HARVEY GIRLS, 1946.

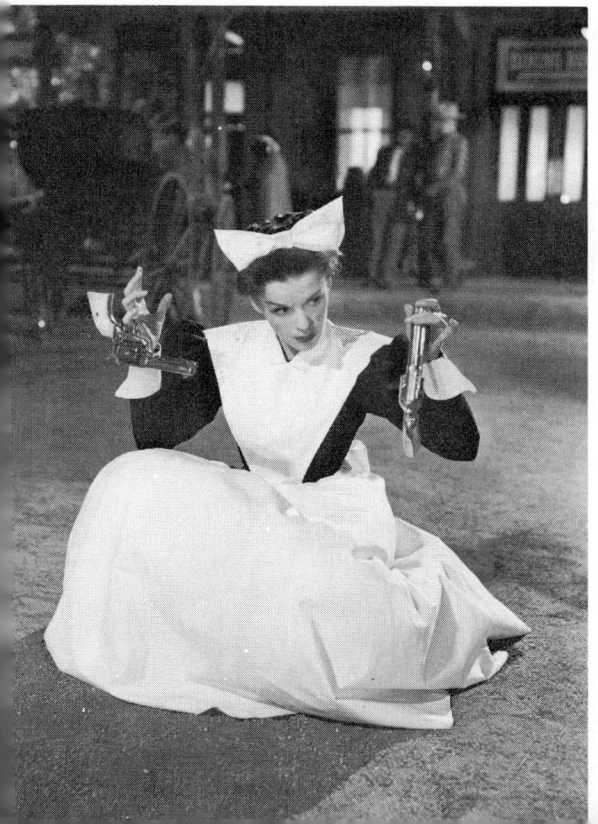

Even in this condition, Deanna Durbin CAN'T HELP SINGING, 1944.

GONE WITH THE WIND, 1939, can not be generalized as a "car[p] film, but it did have some delightful touches of camp, such as Butterfly McQueen telling Vivien Leigh: "Lawsy, we'se got ter have a doctah. Ah don' know nuttin' 'bout birthin' babi[es]

Scarlett is tipsy on brandy. She, therefore, rinsed her mo[uth] with cologne before she decended the staircase to mee[t] Rhett (Clark Gable). However, Rhett knew all about colog[ne]. GONE WITH THE WIND.

After her baby, Scarlett's waist measures 20 inches, to her dismay. Hattie McDaniel reminds her: "Yo done had a baby, Miss Scarlett, and you ain' never goin' to be no eighteen an' a half inches again. Never." GONE WITH THE WIND.

Lotte Lenya (as the Contessa), Vivien Leigh (as a retired stage actress), and Jill St. John (as a starlet in films) appeared in THE ROMAN SPRING OF MRS. STONE, 1961. In this scene, Miss St. John makes remarks to Miss Leigh: "It's such a thrill to meet you, even though I never saw you on the stage. Isn't that terrible?"
Miss Leigh replied: "Not at all. I'm afraid I've never seen you on the screen."

Vivien Leigh did the Charleston in her final film, SHIP OF FOOLS, 1965.

There were enough ladies to give Olivia DeHavilland a little attention in PRINCESS O'ROURKE, 1943.

Katherine Hepburn, in her fantasy world of a poor girl hoping to be elite, has invited Fred MacMurray to dinner with the folks, Ann Shoemaker and Fred Stone. Hattie McDaniel was the maid who chewed gum, kept losing her cap, and served dinner from the wrong side. ALICE ADAMS, 1935.

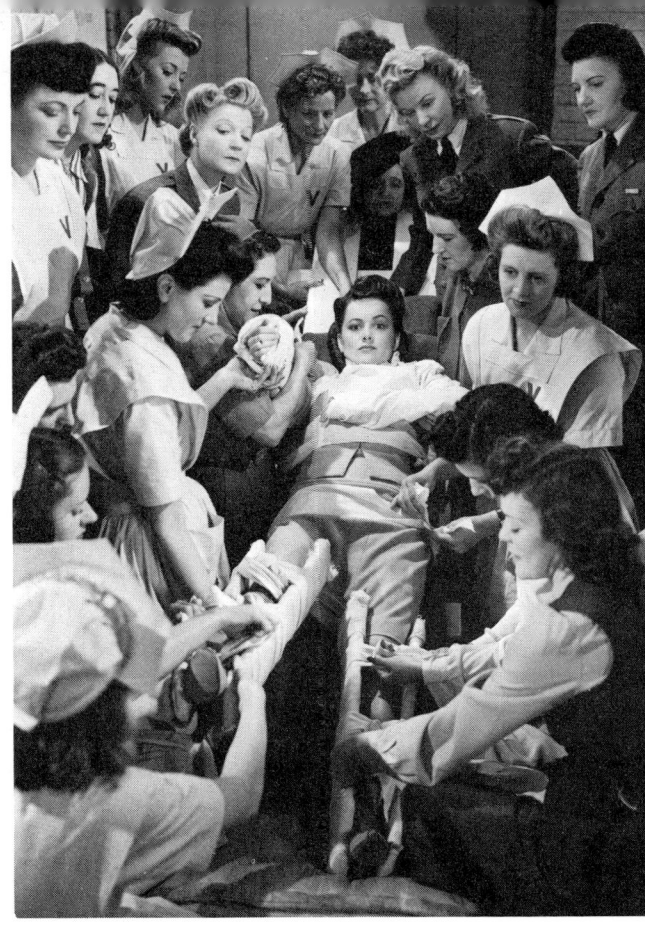

The hotel was all but falling around her from Hitler's bombs, but Ingrid Bergman is telling this headwaiter that that is no reason to delay her evening cocktail in THE YELLOW ROLLS ROYCE, 1965.

Today's audiences might find a different connotation in the title of Norma Shearer's 1930 vehicle, LET US BE GAY.

Geraldine Page (left) had a bit of trouble with her kleptomania prone mother, Una Merkel, in SUMMER AND SMOKE, 1961.

Geraldine Page discusses her "comeback" with Walter Winchell in SWEET BIRD OF YOUTH, 1962.

Geraldine Page (top), Julie Harris (as "Miss Thing"), Elizabeth Hartman, and Tony Bill in YOU'RE A BIG BOY NOW, 1967.

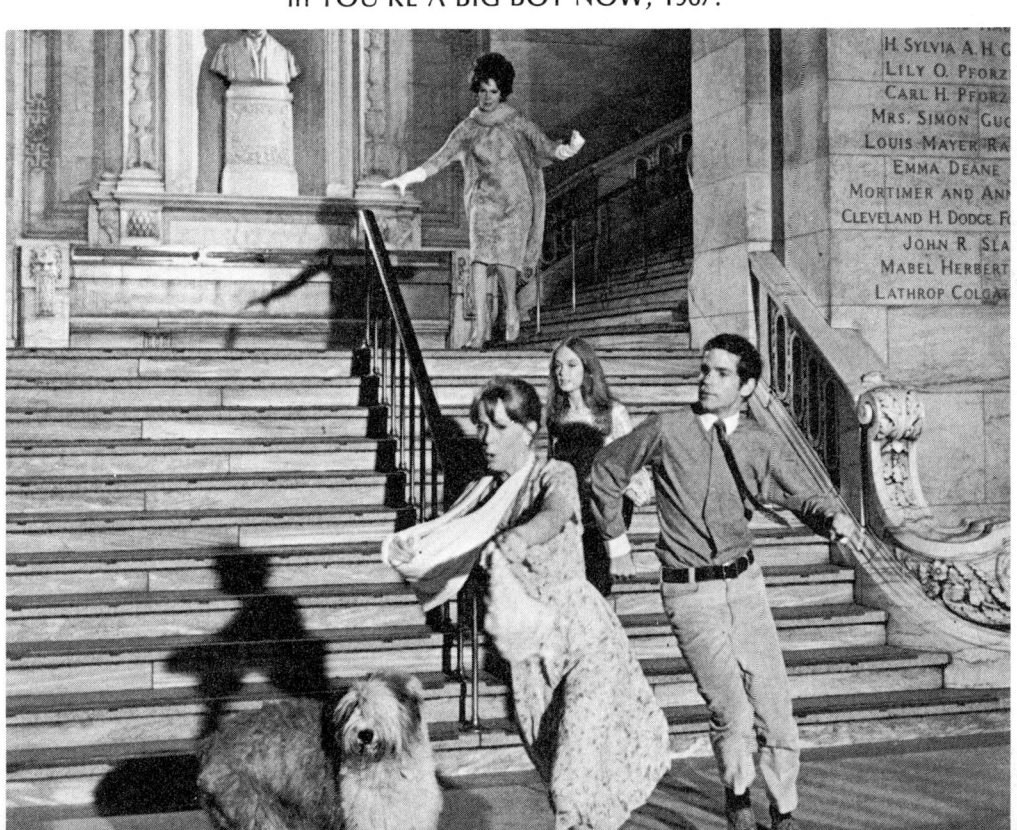

Robert Mitchum, on his birthday, hints at a naughty favor from Shirley MacLaine, his "girlfriend" in TWO FOR THE SEASAW, 1962. He received a negative reply until later when she changed her mind, jumped in bed, and muttered "Oh well, what the hell, Happy Birthday."

Shirley MacLaine has just threatened to close the elevator doors on Jack Lemmon if he pinches her a[gain] in THE APARTMENT, 1960.

Shirley MacLaine was not only Oriental in MY GEISHA, 1[962] but with a little dubbing help she even did selections from the opera "Madama Butterfly."

When Clark Gable returned from World War II, the well remembered ad campaign for ADVENTURE, 1946, stated: "Gable's back, and Garson's got him." But it looks like Joan Blondell also had her hands on him.

Joan Blondell and Henry Jones as the sometimes-drinking married couple who travel with an evangelist's troupe in ANGEL BABY, 1961.

In her early career, Loretta Young ground out many flicks a year. This one is from LOOSE ANKLES, 1930.

You might not recognize these ladies, but they are Jean Arthur and Loretta Young (with Grant Withers) in THE SECOND FLOOR MYSTERY, 1930.

Miss Young's career improved, and in 1948 she won an Oscar for portraying a Swedish domestic named Katie who runs for Congress in THE FARMER'S DAUGHTER, 1947.

Eugene Pallette, Robert Montgomery, and Irene Dunne in UNFINISHED BUSINESS, 1941.

Cary Grant loves Carole Lombard, and Fredric March loves them both in THE EAGLE AND THE HAWK, 19—

Jean Dixon and Carole Lombard in SWING HIGH, SWING LOW, 1937.

Ladies have always had trouble pleasing men with their taste in hats. Mary Beth Hughes and John Barrymore THE GREAT PROFILE, 1940.

Paulette Goddard and Ray Milland in KITTY, 1944.

Audrey Hepburn (as "Holly Golightly") started this fire in BREAKFAST AT TIFFANYS, 1961.

A blonde Elvis Presley meets
a brunette Elvis Presley
in KISSIN' COUSINS, 1964.

Percy Kilbride and Marjorie Main in
MA & PA KETTLE, 1949.

Annette Funicello and Frankie Avalon in
BEACH PARTY, 1963.

Cliff Gorman in THE BOYS IN THE BAND, 1970.

If BEACH PARTY wasn't enough for you, our "stars"
appeared again in BEACH BLANKET BINGO, 1965.

Loretta Young as an artist captured her in September, 1930, for the cover of "Motion Picture Classic."

Although this appears to be a "health-spa" ad, it's actually a well-developed Claudette Colbert for the cover of "The NEW Movie Magazine," in April, 1933.

How else would Olivia DeHavilland spend her time?
The winter edition of "Screen Album" for 1939.

Charlotte Henry is Queen Alice and Edna May Oliver is the red Queen, announcing "Off with her head", in ALICE IN WONDERLAND, 1933.

Julie Andrews in MARY POPPINS, 1964.

This is not the famous shot of Marilyn Monroe in THE SEVEN YEAR ITCH, it's Doris Day in IT'S A GREAT FEELING, 1949.

Poor Doris! Steve Cochran and Ginger Rogers don't know she's there. STORM WARNING, 1951.

Thelma Ritter and Doris Day in PILLOW TALK, 1959.

Cleanliness is next to Godliness. Doris Day in PILLOW TALK, 1959.

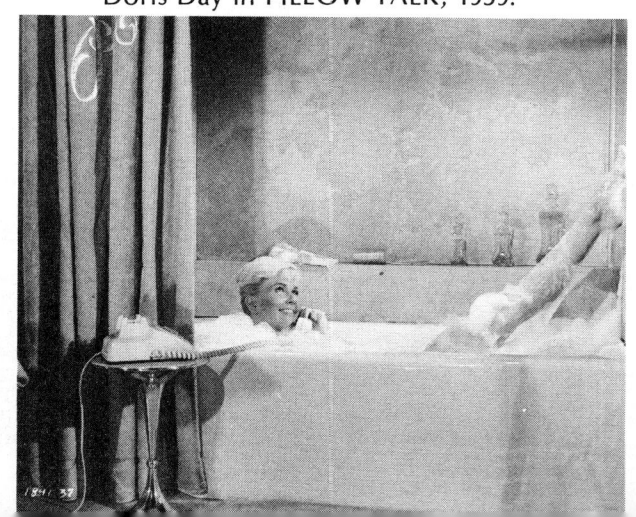

Yet another bath for Doris, in MOVE OVER, DARLING, 1964.

Doris Day in CAPRICE, 1967, with unidentified actor.

"My kitchen sink is so greasy, I have watched bugs slide to their death." Phyllis Diller in EIGHT ON THE LAM, 1967.

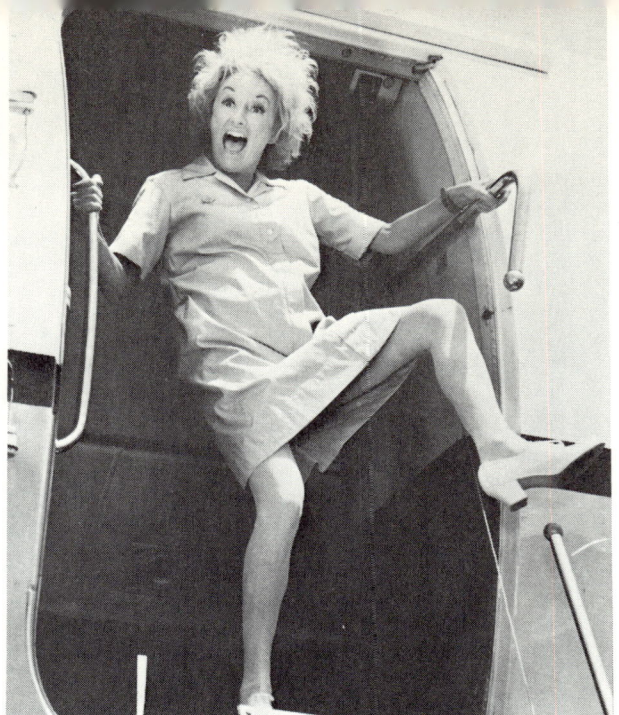

Phyllis Diller in THE PRIVATE NAVY OF SGT. O'FARRELL, 1968.

George Murphy and Alice Faye in YOU'RE A SWEETHEART, 1937.

George Murphy and Shirley Temple (prior to her bid for public office as Congresswoman) in LITTLE MISS BROADWAY, 1938.

Shirley Temple and Jane Withers (subsequently television's lady plumber in the cleanser commercials) in BRIGHT EYES, 1934.

Jane Withers in GIANT, 1956.

Most of the footage in THAT HAGEN GIRL, 1947, involves Ronald Reagan trying to convince Shirley Temple that she is not his illegitimate daughter!

Olivia DeHavilland and Errol Flynn are deeply engrossed with each other, but Ronald Reagan seems to have his mind on bigger and better things. SANTA FE TRAIL, 1940.

Ronald Reagan as a "Marshal" in LAW AND ORDER, 1953.

Four examples of campy art work used to promote a film. First, 1925.

Also from 1932.

1939

Four examples of "movie star ads." First, 1923.

"NOW... I can stand the Public Gaze"... Can You?

Dainty LORETTA YOUNG, First National Star, believes in the health and beauty-giving power of the Sun

CHARM... illusive... appealing... the first requisite of those who wish to be able to stand the public gaze.

It is so easy to be dainty... to appear lovely in other people's eyes... if you keep your skin smooth and free of superfluous hair.

Lounging on the beach with strong sunlight on your bare legs... at dinner with lamplight shining on your bare arms... Wherever you are, whatever you do, you can meet the public gaze with poise if you confirm your daintiness with Del-a-tone.

Removal of under-arm hair lessens perspiration odor.

Easy to use as cold cream, it actually removes hair safely and pleasantly in three minutes or less.

Perfected through our exclusive formula, Del-a-tone Cream is the first and only _white_ cream hair-remover.

Society women, stage and screen stars... renowned for their charm... prefer Del-a-tone Cream to all other methods for removing superfluous hair from under-arm, fore-arm, legs, back of neck and face. It's so *modern*, swift, convenient and so safe.

Send coupon below for trial tube.

Delatone Cream or Powder—at drug and department stores. Or sent prepaid in U. S. in plain wrapper $1. Money back if desired. (Trial tube 10c—use coupon below.) Address Miss Mildred Hadley, The Delatone Company (Established 1908), Dept. 86, The Delatone Bldg., 233 E. Ontario Street, Chicago.

In a recent issue of PHOTOPLAY— JOAN CRAWFORD says:

"I think the stockingless vogue will always last. Tanned legs without hose are most attractive and I shall continue to go stockingless, even with the new styles, except with tailored street dresses."

But don't forget!—Superfluous hair shows up even *more* conspicuously on tanned skins, so be sure to use Del-a-tone before going bare-legged—also before you put on sheer, all-revealing silk stockings.

DEL-A-TONE
The Only _White_ Cream Hair-remover

TRIAL OFFER

Miss Mildred Hadley, The Delatone Company
Dept. 86, Delatone Bldg., 233 E. Ontario Street, Chicago, Ill.
Please send me in plain wrapper prepaid, generous trial tube of Del-a-tone Cream, for which I enclose 10c.
Name....
Street....
City....

1929 sales of Del-a-tone Cream reached a record volume—four times greater than any previous year. Superiority—that's why.

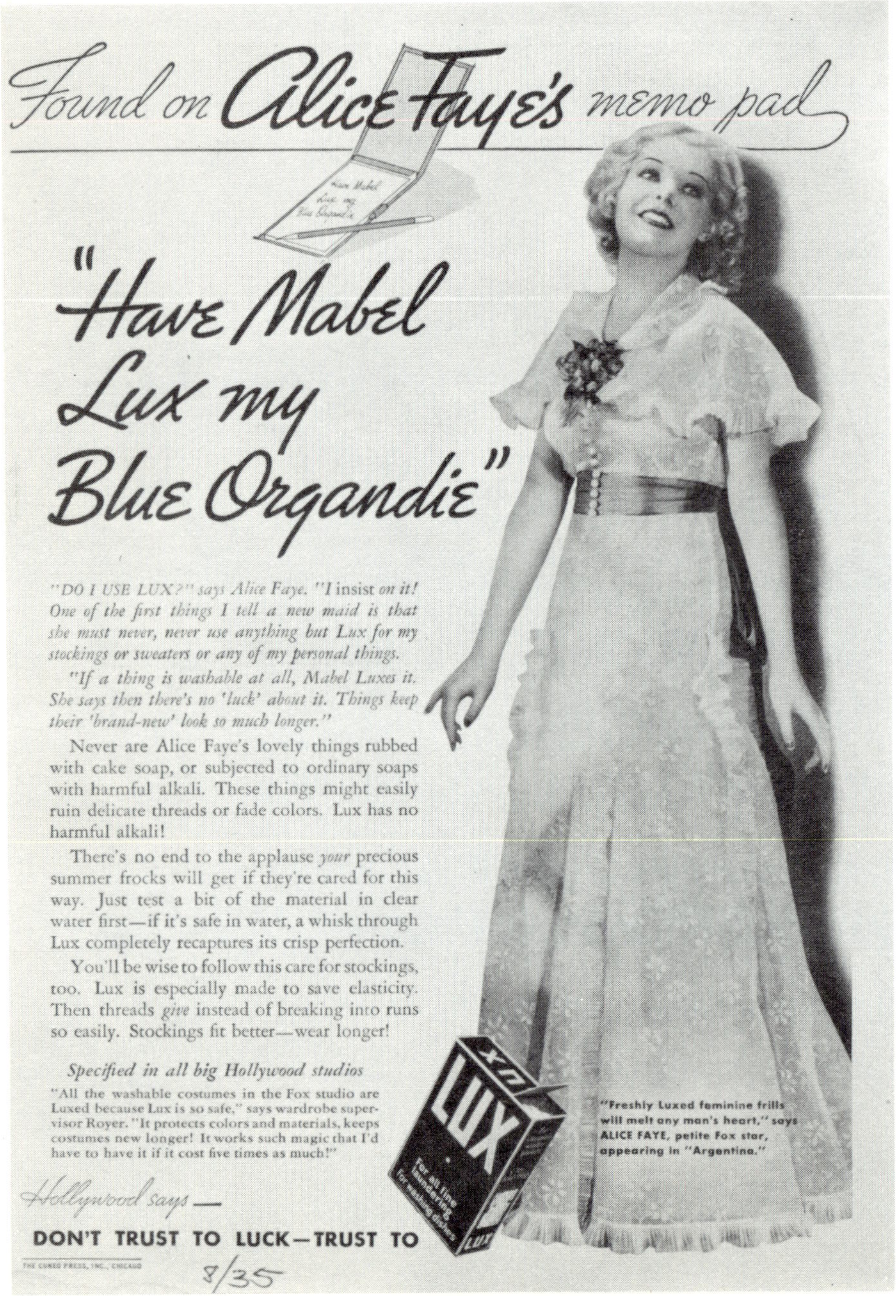

Found on Alice Faye's memo pad

"Have Mabel Lux my Blue Organdie"

"DO I USE LUX?" says Alice Faye. "I insist on it! One of the first things I tell a new maid is that she must never, never use anything but Lux for my stockings or sweaters or any of my personal things.

"If a thing is washable at all, Mabel Luxes it. She says then there's no 'luck' about it. Things keep their 'brand-new' look so much longer."

Never are Alice Faye's lovely things rubbed with cake soap, or subjected to ordinary soaps with harmful alkali. These things might easily ruin delicate threads or fade colors. Lux has no harmful alkali!

There's no end to the applause your precious summer frocks will get if they're cared for this way. Just test a bit of the material in clear water first—if it's safe in water, a whisk through Lux completely recaptures its crisp perfection.

You'll be wise to follow this care for stockings, too. Lux is especially made to save elasticity. Then threads give instead of breaking into runs so easily. Stockings fit better—wear longer!

Specified in all big Hollywood studios "All the washable costumes in the Fox studio are Luxed because Lux is so safe," says wardrobe supervisor Royer. "It protects colors and materials, keeps costumes new longer! It works such magic that I'd have to have it if it cost five times as much!"

"Freshly Luxed feminine frills will melt any man's heart," says ALICE FAYE, petite fox star, appearing in "Argentina."

Hollywood says—
DON'T TRUST TO LUCK—TRUST TO Lux

The favorite of Famous Film Beauties..

Betty Lou POWDER PUFFS 10¢

How they sing the praises of Betty Lou—these captivating stars of screenland! Nothing but the finest may touch their delicately priceless complexions... And so they use *only* Betty Lou Powder Puffs—silky-soft, caressingly fine.

F. W. WOOLWORTH CO 5 AND 10¢ STORES

for sale exclusively

Long before Veronica Lake, Marion Davies sported a "peek-a-boo" hair-do in a publicity still, circa 1933.

Joan Crawford, 1932.

Katharine Hepburn, 1940

Veronica Lake, 1943.

Geraldine Page, 1962.

2

LADIES WHO WERE BORN TO BE BAD

Norma Shearer was a gang moll in LADY OF THE NIGHT, 1925.

Greta Garbo (with Antonio Moreno) couldn't help but make all men her slaves in THE TEMPTRESS, 1926.

Naughty Gloria Swanson,
with her rolled stockings
in FINE MANNERS, 1926.

Mary Pickford
was a chorus girl with a french accent who had stage aspirations in KIKI, 1931, (with Reginald Denny).

1931

In all six of her early talkies, including her first, TARNISHED LADY, 1931 (with Clive Brook) Tallulah Bankhead was a wicked woman, inclined to be promiscuous and double-dealing but always repentant at the final fade-out.

In MY SIN, 1931,
Tallulah was a notorious hussy loose in the Canal Zone and up to some erotic nonsense in a cabaret.

Tallulah Bankhead and Charles Bickford in THUNDER BELOW, 1932.

Wallace Berry tugging on Joan Crawford's garter in GRAND HOTEL, 1932. Joan was a kept woman with a heart of gold.

Miss Crawford as "Sadie Thompson" in RAIN, 1932.

Wallace Berry with Jean Harlow (as "Kitty", the unfaithful wife) in DINNER AT EIGHT, 1933.

In 1934 the Production Code Administration began in Hollywood, and the studios were in a panic regarding morals in
The title of this film with Lionel Barrymore and Jean Harlow got kicked around a bit,
first called BORN TO BE KISSED, then changed to 100% PURE, and finally released as THE GIRL FROM MISSOURI, 193

Billie Burke and Gail Patrick in DOUBTING THOMAS, 1935.

Blondell and Ginger Rogers in BROADWAY BAD, 1933.

Long before she wrote an advice column in "The Catholic Bulletin", Loretta Young was a murderess in MIDNIGHT MARY, 1933.

These ladies were all hostesses at the "Club Intimate."
The word prostitute was then a no-no.
Left to right are Lola Lane, Rosalind Marquis,
Mayo Methot, Bette Davis, Jane Bryan, and Isabel Jewell
in MARKED WOMAN, 1937.

Claudette Colbert also worked her way
into a dance hall in ZAZA, 1938.

Another winner title for Loretta was BORN TO BE BAD, 1934,
with Miss Young as a hardened unwed mother whose baby is adopted by Cary Grant.

Miss Stanwyck appeared in nine films that had the title "lady" in them. These films were called: LADIES OF LEISURE, A LOST LADY, GAMBLING LADY, THE LADY EVE, THE GREAT MAN'S LADY, LADY OF BURLESQUE, THE LADY GAMBLES (not to be confused with GAMBLING LADY), and TO PLEASE A LADY. Lillian Roth (I'LL CRY TOMORROW) is on the left in still another gem title, LADIES THEY TALK ABOUT, 1933.

phanie Bachelor and Barbara Stanwyck (as Dixie, e star-stripper), in LADY OF BURLESQUE, 1943. n the film Miss Stanwyck sang and bounced to: ake it off the E-String, Play it on the G-String."

Cary Grant and Marlene Dietrich, who ranges from being a devoted wife to an unfaithful wife to a nightclub entertainer, in BLOOD VENUS, 1932.

to right from the feather boa are Loretta Young, Marion Martin, Gladys George, and, second from right, the classic "B" girl favorite of all time, Iris Adrian. THE LADY FROM CHEYENNE, 1941.

Veronica Lake and Joan Caulfield are THE SAINTED SISTERS, 1948.

Allure a la Lena Horne in CABIN IN THE SKY, 1943.

Burgess Meredith and Betty Field in OF MICE AND MEN,

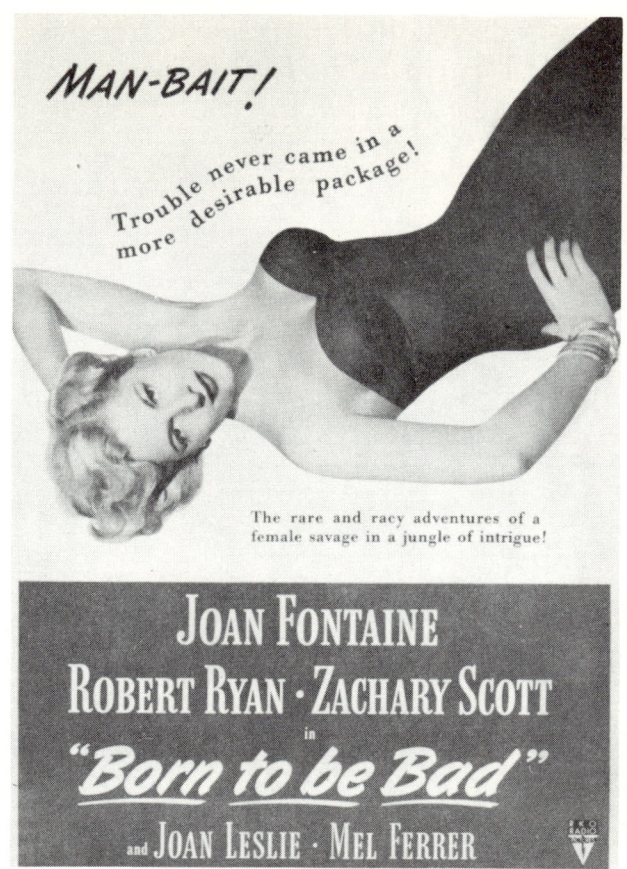
1950

1947

1948

In this scene, Jane Wyman is about to sing a song called "I'm Takin' A Slow Burn Over A Fast Man." If that isn't enough, the film is titled: LET'S DO IT AGAIN, 1953.

In Alfred Hitchcock's excellent suspense film, VERTIGO, 1958, Kim Novak, supposedly dead, pops-up in this "disguise."

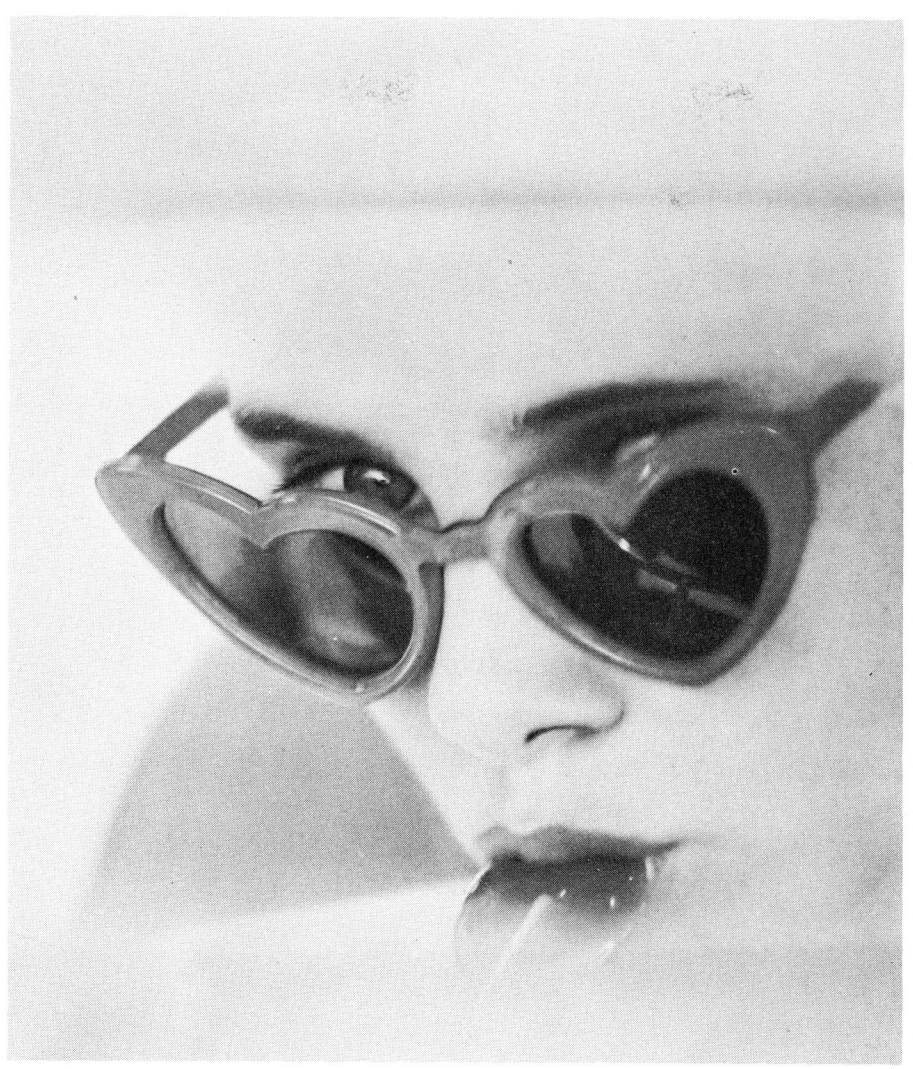

The well known publicity shot for LOLITA, 1962, with Sue Lyon.

Jack Lemmon and Shirley MacLaine in IRMA LA DOUCE, 1963.   Angela Lansbury as the "blowzy blonde" in MISTER BUDDWING, 1966.   Sophia Loren in LADY L, 1966.

Elizabeth Taylor awoke in a strange man's bedroom and ri[nsed] her mouth with booze in the opening scene of BUTTERFIELD 8,

Sylvia Miles undresses Jon Voight while she talks to her friend on the phone in midnight cowboy, 1969.

Jane Fonda as a call-girl in KLUTE, 1971.

Carol Burnett found she forgot the money to pay for her dinner
and had to strip for her supper in WHO'S BEEN SLEEPING IN MY BED?, 1963.

The "Queen of Naughty Ladies", Shelley Winters. THE GREAT GATSBY, 1948.

Shelley Winters in FLAP, 1970.

Michael Caine and Shelley Winters in ALFIE, 1966.

3

THE INCREDIBLE COSTUMES

Theda Bara wore this in SALOME, 1918.

Pola Negri, 1923.

Mae Murray, circa 1918, often posed as though she were the first airplane.

Nita Naldi, 1925.

Miss Murray (as seen in this photo taken in 1923) became well known as the girl with the "bee-stung" lips.

Joan Crawford in a publicity still, 1929.

Lillian Roth (center) and Kay Johnson (right) in two of the wild costumes in MADAME SATAN, 1930.

"Come into the parlor, said the spider to the fly." West and Cary Grant in I'M NO ANGEL, 1933.

A worker could go blind before she finished the detail on almost any of Mae West's gowns. This one is from 1935.

Speaking of spiders, here's Mae again as one in BELLE OF THE NINETIES, 1934.

She also wore this in the same sequence of BELLE OF THE NINETIES.

Irene Dunne wore this little number in THE AWFUL TRUTH, 1937.

Greta Garbo had the busiest clothes of her career in MATA HARI, 1932.

Hedy Lamarr in LADY OF THE TROPICS, 1939.

Carole Lombard's 1934
"skyscraper" dress.

Kay Francis
in MANDALAY, 1934.

Evelyn Brent, circa 1931,
in her butterfly hostess gown.

Loretta Young, Janet Gaynor,
and Constance Bennett
in LADIES IN LOVE, 1936.

Katharine Hepburn's smart 1935 lounging ensemble.

The following two photos are an example of how the studios re-used gowns. Note the black gown in both scenes, here worn by Gladys George (with Norma Shearer) in MARIE ANTIONETTE, 1938

The gown popped up again (minus the lace on the sleeves) on a bit player (with Jeanette Mac Donald) in NEW MOON, 194

Haven't you always wanted a "shoe davenport"? Miss Dietrich in a publicity pose for MANPOWER, 1941.

rlene Dietrich almost holds the record for camp clothes. This one was worn in THE DEVIL IS A WOMAN, 1935.

Miss Dietrich in RANCHO NOTORIOUS, 1952.

An elegant wedding gown for Ginger Rogers in LADY IN THE DARK, 1944.

These "tank-tops" on Joe E. Brown and Preston Foster would be popular today. Ginger Rogers is not standing in front of a ferris wheel, it's her hat!
YOU SAID A MOUTHFUL, 1932.

You'd tilt too from all those beads.
Maria Montez in ARABIAN NIGHTS, 1942.

Merle Oberon wore this in NIGHT IN PARADISE, 1946.

Did someone fling spaghetti at Miss Rogers or is it a Christmas tree gown? Ginger is with Walter Pigeon in WEEKEND AT THE WALDORF, 1945.

"I, Yi, Yi, Yi, Yi, We Like You Very Much." Carmen Miranda, 1942.

Mickey Rooney as Carmen Miranda
in BABES ON BROADWAY, 1941.

Harold Lloyd and Frances Ramsden
in MAD WEDNESDAY, 1947.

Doris Day
in THE GLASS BOTTOM BOAT, 1966.

Gloria Swanson
in a publicity shot for SUNSET BOULEVARD, 1950.

Oscar Levant and, yep, it's Doris Day.
ROMANCE ON THE HIGH SEAS, 1948.

Rosalind Russell, in addition to being a very talented actress,
was also known as one of Hollywood's leading clotheshorses.

And here she is in person, designer Edith Head.

Robert Mitchum and Shirley MacLaine in WHAT A WAY TO GO?, 1964. Miss MacLaine's gowns were designed by Edith H

Barbra Streisand and George Segal have six hands in THE OWL AND THE PUSSYCAT, 1970.

John Phillip Law and Jane Fonda in BARBARELLA,

The great stone face,
Buster Keaton in A FUNNY THING HAPPENED ON THE WAY TO THE FORUM, 1966.

Gloria Swanson, 1919,
opens the following galaxy of female and male impersonators.

Stan Laurel and Oliver Hardy and their "wives" in TWICE TWO, 1933.

Eddie Cantor and Charlotte Greenwood
PALMY DAYS, 1931.

Marlene Dietrich, 1930.

William Powell in LOVE CRAZY, 1941.

In this scene May Robson has just asked Cary Grant what he's doing in Katharine Hepburn's negligee, and Cary announced: "I've suddenly gone gay." BRINGING UP BABY, 1938.

Marlene Dietrich in SEVEN SINNERS,

Joan Davis and Jack Haley in
GEORGE WHITE'S SCANDALS OF 1945.

Raquel Welch in MYRA BRECKINRIDGE, 1970.

Annabella
(who in real life was Mrs. Tyrone Power)
in WINGS OF THE MORNING, 1937.

Tony Curtis and Jack Lemmon on the set of SOME LIKE IT HOT, 1959.
Mr. Lemmon recently reminisced that production on the film was held up for a half day because Marilyn fell in love with one of his dresses and swiped it!

Bob Hope in THE LEMON DROP KID, 1950.

Jack Lemmon and Joe E. Brown are about to do the Tango in SOME LIKE IT HOT.

Joe E. Brown in SHUT MY BIG MOUTH, 1941.

Paul Lynde and Eric Fleming in THE GLASS BOTTOM BOAT, 1966.

Six football players from the Detroit Lions were starred in PAPER LION, 1968.

George Sanders in THE KREMLIN LETTER, 1970.

4

THE SEX GODS AND GODDESSES

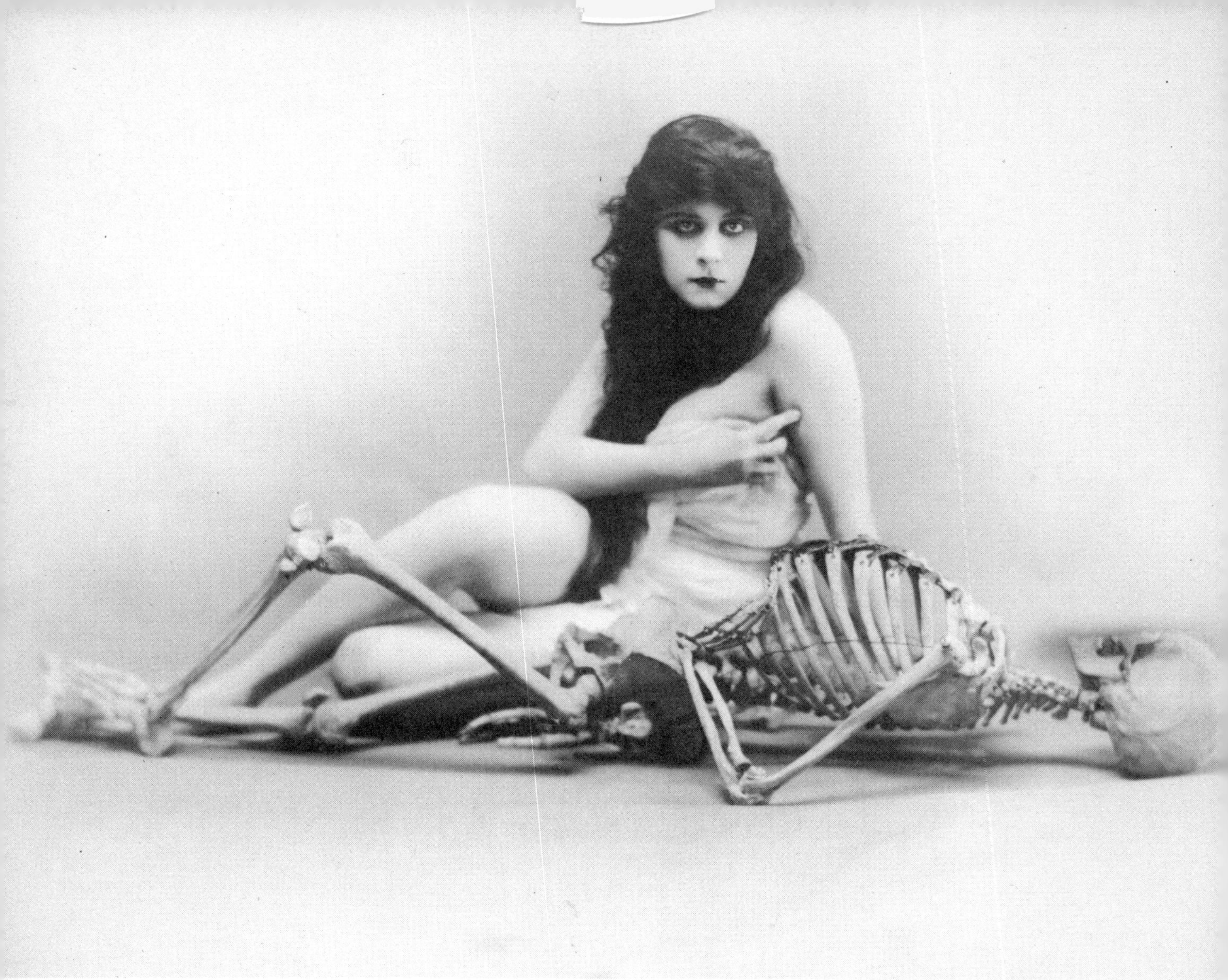

"Kiss me, my Fool" is a famous subtitle from Theda Bara's first film, A FOOL THERE WAS, 1915. This shot is a publicity still for the film, and press publicity had the public believing that Theda was born near the Sphinx on an oasis in the Sahara. She was actually little Theodosia Goodman from Cincinnati.

One may wonder why Theda always seemed to have her arms in th[e air]. Possibly in despair over the fact that this film, THE SOUL OF BUDD[HA], 1918, had been written by none other than the "vamp" herself.

Poor Theda. In real life she was as blind as a bat, and at the studio she couldn't see the chalk marks that outlined the camera's range. Here she is, only one arm up this time, in LA BELLE RUSSE, 1919.

The reverse of this photo states that the scene is from THE LIGHT, 1919. "A Theda Bara *Super* Production." Theda made forty-one movies between 1915 and her final appearance in 1926, possibly due to the fact that she had nothing else to do, since her contract stated that if she were to keep the public's idea of "vamp," she was not to be seen anywhere in public.

Rudolph Valentino, circa 1924, the great lover to end all great lovers. He became the idol of women everywhere.

The flapper of the Jazz age, who became famous as Hollywood's "It" girl, Clara Bow, 1926.

The first "swimming Queen of the screen," Annette Keller in NEPTUNE' DAUGHTER, 1914.

If you're going to star in an epic about the air-force, then you're entitled to wear an airplane on your hat. Clara Bow in WINGS, 1927.

arlene Dietrich's famous legs had not quite reached their peak of fame when she posed for her first American film, MOROCCO, 1930.

Miss Dietrich's legs were painted gold in KISMET, 1944.

Buster Crabbe and Ida Lupino found what they were looking for in SEARCH FOR BEAUTY, 1934.

And the never-surpassed swimming queen, Esther Williams, on the set of RAW WIND IN EDEN, 1958. In this outfit the RAW WIND may creep up from behind.

Buster Crabbe in FLASH GORDON'S TRIP TO MARS, 1938.

Cary Grant and Randolph Scott at their Santa Monica beach home in 1935.

The famous World War II pin-up girl, Betty Grable.

The censor would not allow Clark Gable to unfold his hand in this publicity still with Joan Crawford for STRANGE CARGO, 1940.

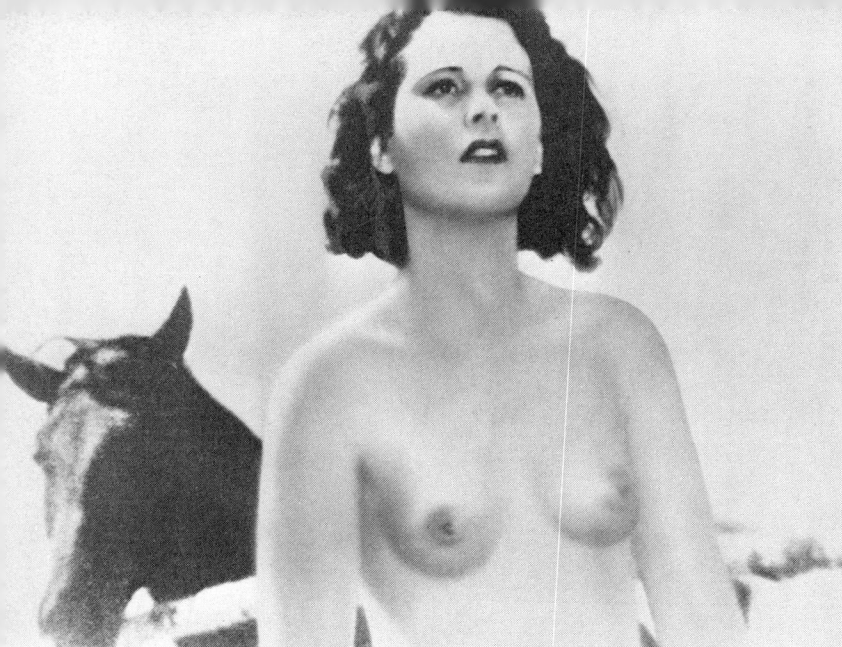

Several years before Hedy Lamarr came to California to become a big star overnight, she appeared in this stunning outfit in ECSTASY, 1933.

A few years after she got to sunny California, Hedy appeared as a jungle temptress in WHITE CARGO, 1942. She made her entrance in the film by announcing "I am Tondelayo."

A famous portrait of Ann Sheridan, circa 1940, when she was labeled Hollywood's "Oomph" girl.

Men melted when Rita sang "Put The Blame On Mame" in GILDA, 1946.

Jane Russell *started* as a star. Not only that, second contract with Howard Hughes, signed in 1955, ovides a salary until 1977, whether she works or not. e has seldom appeared on film since 1957.) This is one of the publicity poses for THE OUTLAW, 1943.

Lana Turner, posed on the set of THE POSTMAN ALWAYS RINGS TWICE, 1946.

ss Harlow in 1936 at the height of her tardom as the reigning sex Goddess.

Jean's ultimate successor was Marilyn Monroe. No one has been able to top Marilyn's star quality. HOW TO MARRY A MILLIONAIRE, 1953.

Marilyn Monroe in
THERE'S NO BUSINESS LIKE SHOW BUSINESS, 1954.

Marilyn's famous pose for THE SEVEN YEAR ITCH, 19

Kim Novak as JEANNE EAGLES, 1957.

[Y]ou could not be a love goddess without at least one [bub]ble bath somewhere along the line. Kim Novak, 1957.

Jayne Mansfield in PROMISES! PROMISES!, 1963.

Mamie Van Doren made it to the top, but in "B" pictures which usually had no lasting quality. THE BEAT GENERATION, 1959.

If you were two little old ladies and Tarzan wandered out of a bush, you'd be shocked too. Buster Crabbe in KING OF THE JUNGLE, 1933.

Maureen O'Sullivan and Johnny Weissmuller in TARZAN, THE APE MAN, 1932.

Just as the female temptress had a larger bosom with each cinema decade, the Tarzans got bigger and even slightly exaggerated too! Mike Henry in TARZAN AND THE JUNGLE BOY, 1968.

The he-man, Steve Reeves, in HERCULES UNCHAINED, 1960.

To bring us up to date, the girl who arrived too late for the "star system." Raquel Welch in BANDOLERO, 1968.

5

THE HORROR FILMS
(that made you shake from either fear or laughter)

If you ever meet anyone who has been confronted by a monster,
ask him if it's standard procedure to lie down and watch.
Lon Chaney, Sr. is the PHANTOM OF THE OPERA, 1925.

Some days it just doesn't pay to get up
and plan a simple wedding.
Mae Clarke and Boris Karloff in FRANKENSTEIN, 1931.

Elsa Lanchester (with Boris Karloff as the monster)
doesn't appear to be thrilled
about becoming THE BRIDE OF FRANKENSTEIN, 19

Bela Lugosi in DRACULA, 1931.

Miriam Hopkins didn't mind an occasional fondle,
she just didn't care for Fredric March in DR. JEYKLL AND MR. HYDE, 1932.

Night time is the right time.
Bela Lugosi and Carol Borland in MARK OF THE VAMPIRE, 1935.

Bruce Cabot, Fay Wray,
and Robert Armstrong
had better than orchestra seats
for New York's *smash* opening
of KING KONG, 1933.

Maidie Norman as Elvira, Joan Crawford as Blanche Hudson, and Bette Davis portraying the title role in WHAT EVER HAPPENED TO BABY JANE? Slatern Jane has just entered Blanche's room, announcing: "I was cleanin the cage. The bird flew out the window."

"But you *are* in that wheelchair, Blanche, you *are*. And you aren't ever 'gonna leave it, either." Bette Davis and Joan Crawford in WHAT EVER HAPPENED TO BABY JANE?, 1962.

Upon learning that Johnson's Liquor Store will not fill *her* order, Jane impersonates Blanche's voice, actually dubbed in the film by Joan Crawford. "After all we do pay our bills, don't we?" She remembered to order everything except a Pepsi for Blanche in WHAT EVER HAPPENED TO BABY JANE?

Everyone tried to create a feud between Bette Davis and Joan Crawford on the WHAT EVER HAPPENED TO BABY JANE but the main "feud" was on film. It also recouped its cost in 11 days, and landed 5 Academy Award nominations. Bette, incidentally, designed and applied her own make-up for this role

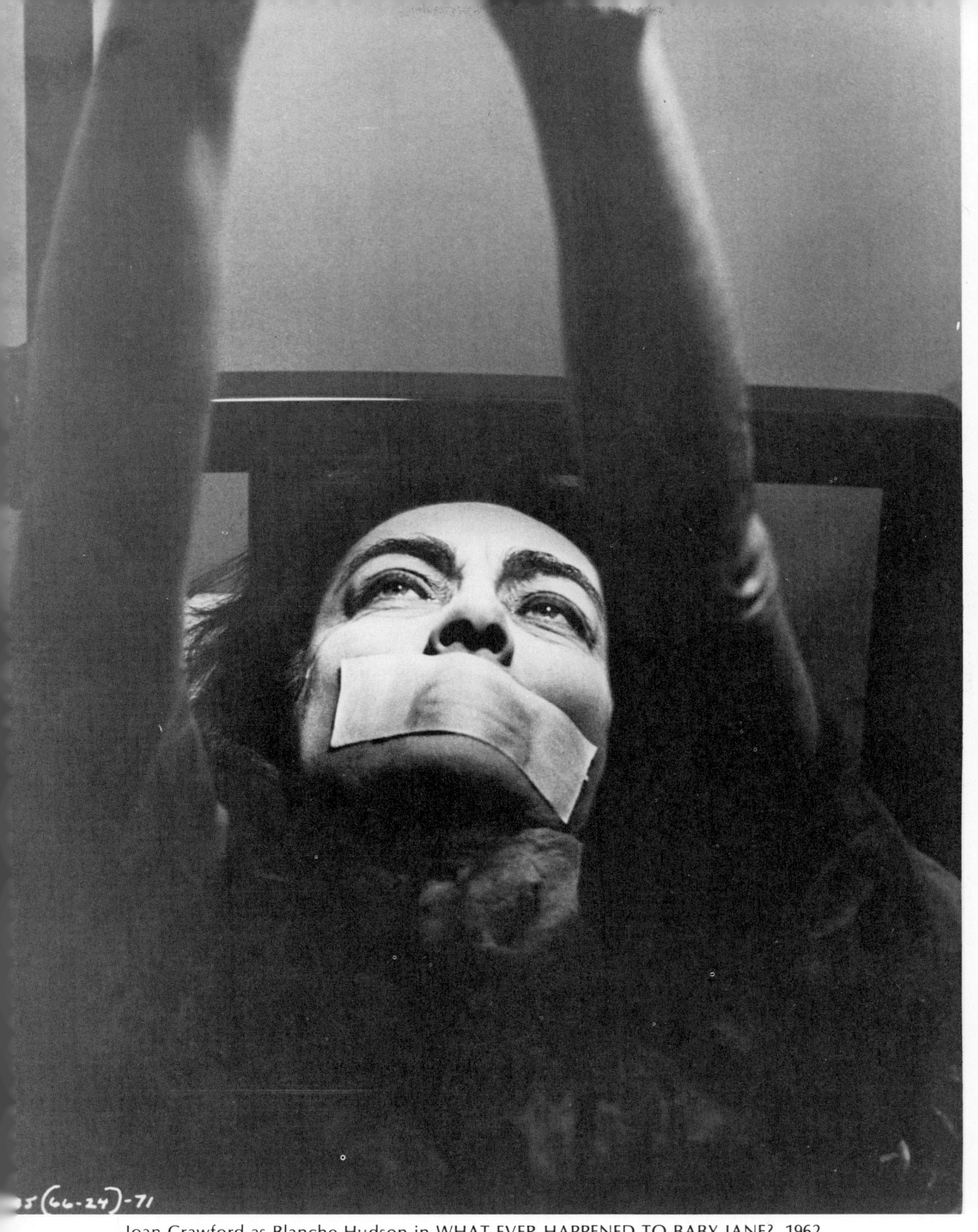

Joan Crawford as Blanche Hudson in WHAT EVER HAPPENED TO BABY JANE?, 1962.
This film's success started the following wave of horror films in recent years.

Geraldine Page delighted in bumping off her housekeepers, burying them in her garden, and each time planting a tree over them. in WHAT EVER HAPPENED TO AUNT ALICE?, 1969.

A never-chubbier Shelley Winters is Helen in WHAT'S THE MATTER WITH HELEN?, 19

Geraldine Page and Ruth Gordon
in WHAT EVER HAPPENED TO AUNT ALICE?, 1969.

Bette Davis played twins twice in her career, and neither set cared too much for her sister. This time "Eadie" is about to give "Margaret" a headache in DEAD RINGER, 1964.

Joan, as the axe-murderess, is about to take care of George Kennedy. Another of her victims was Mitchell Cox, who in real life was Vice President of the Pepsi-Cola Company! STRAIGHT JACKET.

Crime does not pay. Tallulah bids a last farewell to her son, which was a smart thing to do since there's a knife in her back. DIE! DIE! MY DARLING!, 1965. Asked why she appeared in such a role after a long screen absence, Miss Bankhead replied: "The money, dahling. Not that I'm poor but I do enjoy the Rolls-Royce, and I won't go to London without staying at the Ritz."

The point in the film has been reached where Olivia DeHavilland pets crazed Bette Davis like a kitten and delivers the title line: HUSH . . . HUSH, SWEET CHARLOTTE, 1965.

Agnes Moorehead was a hoot as a slovenly housekeeper, with Bette Davis as Charlotte, in HUSH . . . HUSH, SWEET CHARLOTTE.

Joan Crawford was John Ireland's lover in I SAW WHAT YOU DID, 1965, but since nothing lasts forever, look what happened to her.

Olivia DeHavilland's real life sister, Joan Fontaine, also got on the horror bandwagon, even if she did have only one Oscar to her sisters two. Joan appears to be wearing a fox-fur, but it's nothing more than a couple of monster hands. THE DEVIL'S OWN, 1967.

In 1951 Kim Hunter won an Oscar for A STREETCAR NAMED DESIRE. Here she is getting drunk on champagne in ESCAPE FROM THE PLANET OF THE APES, 1971.

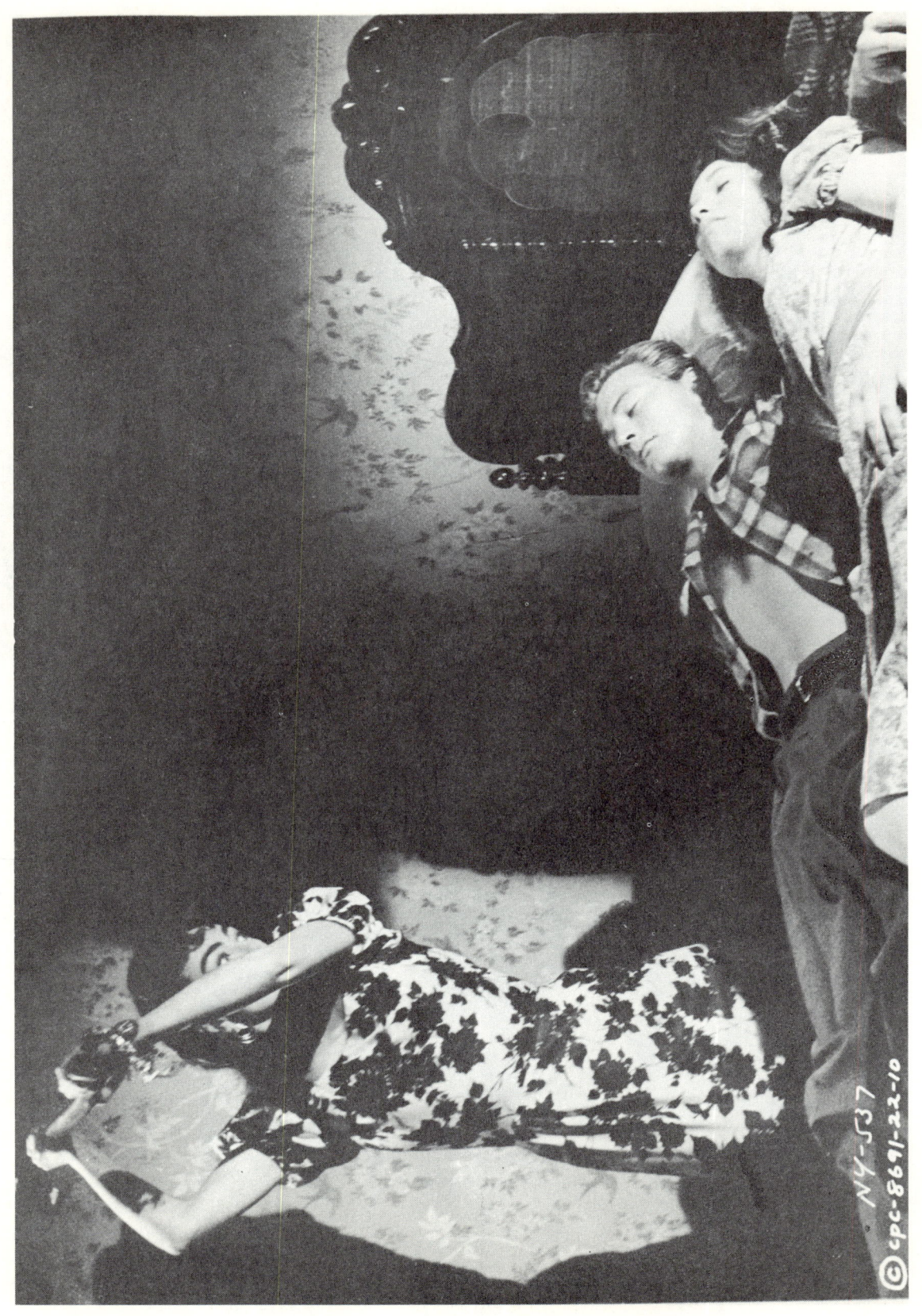

Joan Crawford has just returned home to find her husband abed with another woman. And, throughout STRAIGHT JACKET, 1964, we hear this little chant. "Lucy Harbin Took An Axe, And Gave Her Husband Forty Whacks." Not only that, you could always tell a murder was about to happen when Lucy's bracelets started to jingle.

6

THE FABULOUS MUSICALS

A silent film could have a musical number if it felt like it. Here is Gloria Swanson and a bevy of beauties in HER GILDED CAGE, 1922, five years before the advent of "talkies."

...n the help of the mighty pipe organ, John Gilbert could dance the famous ...z with Mae Murray in THE MERRY WIDOW, 1925.

Not only were "Talkies" here, but so was "100% Natural Color." And 1929 "color" was something else.

1931.

Busby Berkeley is directing Eddie Cantor in the proper art of kissing Ruth Etting while the "Goldwyn Girls" watch in ROMAN SCANDALS, 1933.

Eddie Cantor and Lyda Roberti in THE KID FROM SPAIN, 1932.

If you were a big star you not only had to learn to act, but also how to play the violin. Alice Faye and Tyrone Power in ALEXANDER'S RAGTIME BAND, 1938.

Mickey Rooney, his violin, and Judy Garland in BABES IN ARMS, 1939.

Now here's someone who *could* play the violin. Jack Benny (with Bette Davis) in HOLLYWOOD CANTEEN, 1944.

Finally, Ruby Keeler with her friends in the "Shadow Waltz" number from GOLD DIGGERS OF 1933.

Olivia DeHavilland and Jane Wyman with their violins in MY LOVE CAME BACK, 1940.

ce director Busby Berkeley became famous through his gned production numbers. This fantastic set is for the A Waterfall" number from FOOTLIGHT PARADE, 1933.

Busby directed many famous musical numbers. His favorite was "Lullaby of Broadway," with Dick Powell and Wini Shaw way up there at the right) in GOLD DIGGERS OF 1935.

Ricardo Cortez, Dick Powell, Al Jolson, and Dolores Del Rio in WONDER BAR, 1935.

The "Tip-Toe Thru The Tulips" number from

A few of the dancing girls in the sumptuous garden fete scene from a "Norma Talmadge Starring Vehicle," DU BARRY, WOMAN OF PASSION, 1930.

One may wonder how a studio could ever afford this

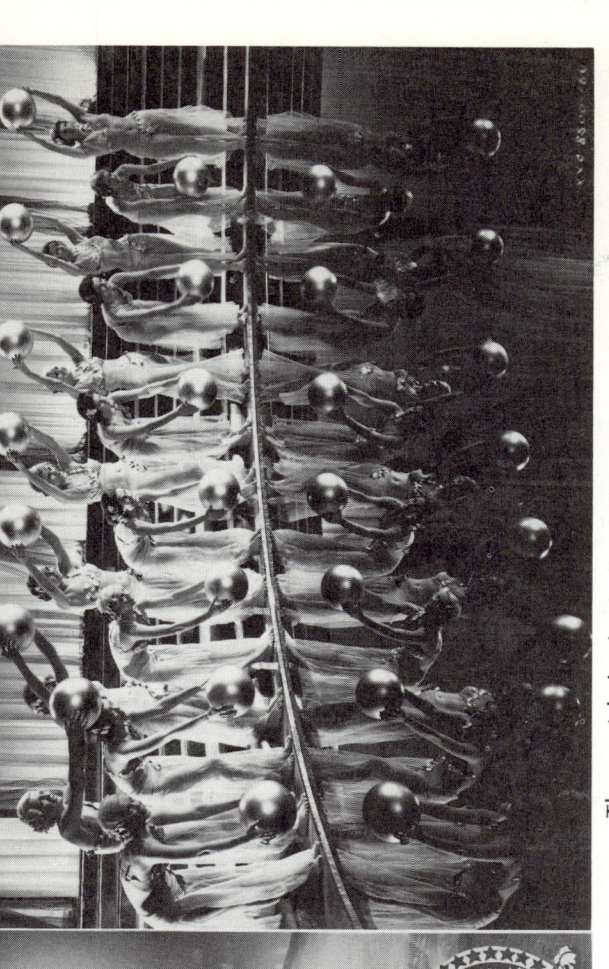

These girls had a ball in BROADWAY THRU A KEYHOLE, 1933.

Samuel Goldwyn's "Glorious Goldwyn Cover Girls" in THE GOLDWYN FOLLIES, 1938.

These girls could never get TOO MUCH HARMONY, 1933.

Dance-hall girls in Mae West's films were usually chubby, as that made Miss West look slimmer. BELLE OF THE NINETIES, 1934.

Sterling Holloway, Priscilla Lane, Lee Dixon, Rosemary Lane, Dick Powell, Mabel Todd, and Ted Hea in VARSITY SHOW, 1937.

Ruth Chatterton was an opera star in SARAH AND SON, 1930. She was coached for this role by Mme. Ernestine Schumann-heink.

Maurice Chevalier in the "Sweeping the Clouds Away" number in PARAMOUNT ON PARADE, 1930. The girls are about to grab brooms and start sweeping.

A publicity shot for SITTING PRETTY, 1933.

Helen Kane as a singing teacher in PARAMOUNT ON PARADE. Everytime she asked a question the kiddies answered: "Boop-Boop-A-Doop."

Also in PARAMOUNT ON PARADE was Nancy Carroll who made her entrance by coming out of a big shoe. She sang "Dancing To Save My Sole."

Joan Blondell and chorus in the "All is Fair In Love and War" number from GOLD DIGGERS OF 1937.

Jeanette MacDonald was in this production number for PARAMOUNT ON PARADE.

Marion Davies never looked lovelier than in the "I'll Sing You A Thousand Love Songs" number from CAIN AND MABEL, 19

Douglas Fairbanks, Sr. and Bebe Daniels in the hysterical "There's No Low-Down Lower Than That" number from REACHING FOR THE MOON, 1931.

Joan Crawford in THE HOLLYWOOD REVUE OF 19

Marie Dressler, Bessie Love, and Polly Moran in THE HOLLYWOOD REVUE OF 1929.

Joan Crawford and Fred Astaire in DANCING LADY, 1933.

Claudette Colbert in TORCH SINGER, 1933.

LOIS WILSON still stands for cleaner pictures. She is all dressed up for the song "White Wings They Never Grow Weary." Lois wears this costume in "Broadway Nights," the story of a cabaret girl who keeps the Great White Way white.

Ruby Keeler, after three years of marital bliss and idleness, will soon be tapping her toes in her first cinema, "42nd St."

Mrs. Al Jolson goes to work

From the November, 1932 issue of *Vanity Fair*.

Ruby Keeler (foreground on steps)
and her girlfriends in DAMES.

Una Merkel, Ruby Keeler, George E. Stone, Warner Baxter,
and Ginger Rogers in FORTY SECOND STREET.
Memorable line: Bebe Daniels, unable to "go on" because of a broken ankle tel
Ruby Keeler: "Now you go out there and be so swell that it will make me hate you

In the center of all those girls is Busby Berkeley, on set for DAMES.

The girls fit a puzzle together in a musical sequence from DAMES, 1934, which turns out to be a picture of "the star"—Ruby Keeler.

1937.

Miss Keeler in GO INTO YOUR DANCE, 1935.

Dick Powell and an always shy Ruby Keeler in FLIRTATION WALK, 1934.

1941.

Ginger Rogers opened GOLD DIGGERS OF 1933 dressed in this costume. She sang "We're In The Money" in Pig-Latin.

inger is singing "Music Makes Me" (with Gene Raymond) in FLYING DOWN TO RIO, 1933.

Jack Haley and Ginger Rogers in SITTING PRETTY, 1933.

Mae West singing "They Call Me Sister Honky Tonk" in I'M NO ANGEL, 19

James Ellison, Beulah Bondi, and Ginger Rogers are not aware that Beulah's stuffy husband, Charles Coburn (right) has just walked in to find them doing "The Big Apple" in VIVACIOUS LADY, 1938.

...reme camp was Mae singing selections from the opera "Samson and Delilah," in GOIN' TO TOWN, 1935.

Ginger didn't impress Fred at all with her "Yama-Yama" dance in THE STORY OF VERNON AND IRENE CASTLE, 1939.

Unusual for Mae was a black wig, from the "Fifi" musical sequence in EVERY DAY'S A HOLIDAY, 1938.

George Raft's early career included dancing, and Carole Lombard had a go at it, too. BOLERO, 1934.

Jeanette MacDonald singing the title song in SAN FRANCISCO, 1936.

Jeanette MacDonald in THE LOTTERY BRIDE, 1930.

Jeanette MacDonald in LOVE ME TONIGHT, 19

Ray Bolger and Jeanette MacDonald in SWEETHEARTS, 1938.

Slim Summerville, Shirley Temple, and Guy Kibbee in CAPTAIN JANUARY, 1936.

Jack Haley, Shirley Temple, and Alice Faye
in the "Military Man" number from THE POOR LITTLE RICH GIRL, 1936.

Shirley Temple and Bill Robinson in THE LITTLEST REBEL, 1935.

In EVERY NIGHT AT EIGHT, 1935, Alice Faye, Frances Langford, and Patsy Kelly, known as "The Swannee Sisters," sang such delights as: "If you have to take it, take it easy."

Alice Faye is singing "Let's Go Slumming on Park Avenue" in ON THE AVENUE, 1937.

Alice Faye, Joan Davis, and Marjorie Weaver sang "Who Stole The Jam?" in SALLY, IRENE AND MARY. The song had lyrics such as: "Momma wants to know who stole the jam, who made that mess, Momma's gonna kick some teeth in, if you don't confess."

Joan Davis and Gregory Ratoff did a spanish tango in SALLY, IRENE AND MARY.

George Burns and Gracie Allen in COLLEGE HOLIDAY, 1936.

Fred Astaire, Gracie Allen, and George Burns in "Fun-House" number in A DAMSEL IN DISTRESS, 1937.

Edward Everett Horton listened while Gracie Allen sang "You're A Natural" in COLLEGE SWING, 1938. On the dusty road, and in a white chiffon dress, with cows in the background yet, Gracie kicked up her heels doing a dance to the car radio.

On her recent album recordings, Marlene Dietrich introduces the song "Johnny" by saying "I have to sing it in the original language, because no English lyrics were ever written for it." This is how she looked while singing "Johnny" in English, in THE SONG OF SONGS, 1933.

Marlene sang "See What the Boys in the Back Room Will Have" in DESTRY RIDES AGAIN, 1939.

In BLONDE VENUS, 1932, Marlene Dietrich made her entrance to sing "Hot Voodoo" dressed as an ape. When she disrobed, she emerged like this and went right into her number.

Jesse Matthews in IT'S LOVE AGAIN, 1936.

Ethel Merman in ANYTHING GOES, 1935.

Even Jean Harlow tried her hand at a musical. Here she is going to town in RECKLESS, 1935.

Ethel Merman in STRIKE ME PINK, 1935.

If you can't imagine Olivia DeHavilland singing opera, then see ANTHONY ADVERSE, 1936.

Paul Robeson, Irene Dunne, Hattie McDaniel, and Helen Morgan in SHOWBOAT, 1936.

Leah Ray (seated) and Joan Davis in THIN ICE, 1937.

Even Charles Laughton and Vivien Leigh were once in a musical number. SIDEWALKS OF LONDON, 1938.

Miss Raye as "Babe" in COLLEGE HOLIDAY, 1937.

Ben Blue and Martha Raye kept on truckin' in THE BIG BROADCAST OF 1938.

Martha Raye sang "Mr. Paganini" in her first feature film, and the song became her trademark. Bob Burns helped out on the "Bazooka" in RHYTHM ON THE RANGE, 1936.

Martha Raye in one of her great routines while singing in THE BOYS FROM SYRACUSE, 1940.

In this dress and snood, Ann Sheridan sang "Love Isn't Born, It's Made" in THANK YOUR LUCKY STARS, 1943.

Hattie McDaniel and Willie Best in the "Ice Cold K number from THANK YOUR LUCKY STARS.

Ann Sheridan, Alexis Smith, and Jane Wyman in THE DOUGHGIRLS, 1944.

In THANK YOUR LUCKY STARS Bette Davis san "They're Either Too Young or Too Old," referrin the men who had not gone to war. Enough fun in she followed the song with a "jitterbug."

Olivia DeHavilland, George Tobias, and Ida Lupino in THANK YOUR LUCKY STARS.

Jackie Coogan and Betty Grable with Skinnay Ennis and his Orchestra in the hysterical title number from COLLEGE SWING, 1938.

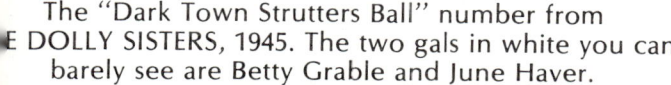

The "Dark Town Strutters Ball" number from THE DOLLY SISTERS, 1945. The two gals in white you can barely see are Betty Grable and June Haver.

Alice Faye, Billy Gilbert, and Betty Grable in TIN PAN ALLEY, 1940.

Betty Grable in SWEET ROSIE O'GRADY, 1943.

Rita Hayworth in MY GAL SAL, 1942.

Paulette Goddard, Dorothy Lamour, and Veronica Lake are singing "A Sweater, A Sarong, and A Peek-a-Boo Bang," in STAR SPANGLED RHYTHM, 1942.

Jack Oakie, Shirley Temple (on the "road" to maturity) and Charlotte Greenwood in YOUNG PEOPLE, 1940.

Mickey Rooney and Judy Garland impersonated Franklin D. and Eleanor Roosevelt in the "God's Country" number from BABES IN ARMS, 1939.

Busby Berkeley's dance sensations continued into the 1940's. This time Mickey Rooney and Judy Garland show they "Got Rhythm" in GIRL CRAZY, 1943.

Miss Garland in the "Minnie From Trinidad" number from ZIEGFELD GIRL, 1941. The lyrics went: "Minnie came to Hollywood to be a star, and they changed her name to Minnie Lamarr."

In THOUSANDS CHEER, 1943, Judy is singing "The Joint is Really Jumpin' Down at Carnegie Hall."

Judy in "The Interview," a musical sketch about a big star and her future plans, in ZIEGFELD FOLLIES, 1946.

"Strange Things Are Happening To This Heart of Mine" sang Marlene Dietrich in THE LADY IS WILLING, 1941.

Kate Smith singing "God Bless America" in THIS IS THE ARMY, 1943.

Carmen Miranda visited the set of BABES ON BROADWAY, 1941, with Busby Berkeley and Mickey Rooney.

Lupe Velez in MEXICAN SPITFIRE'S ELEPHANT, 1942.

Up on the steps doing who-knows-what is Jeanette MacDonald in BROADWAY SERENADE, 1939.

Betty Hutton was always "truckin around," in HAPPY-GO-LUCKY, 1942.

Ann Southern and Jack Carson in APRIL SHOWERS, 1948.

For the most famous sister-act in nightclubs and on records, the Andrews Sisters made relatively few films during their "heyday" in the 1940's. Here they are sockin' it to the celluloid audience in HER LUCKY NIGHT, 1945.

Kathryn Grayson in THE KISSING BANDIT, 1948.

Ann Miller had no shame in letting everyone know who the Queen of the streets was in EASTER PARADE, 1948.

George Murphy, Constance Moore, Eddie Cantor, and a rather buxom Joan Davis in SHOW BUSINESS, 1944.

Donald O'Connor, Madge Blake (impersonating Louella Parsons), Gene Kelly, and Jean Hagen in the classic take-off on the 1920's, SINGING IN THE RAIN, 1952.

Gene Kelly and Jean Hagen portrayed silent screen stars named Don Lockwood and Lina Lamont in SINGING IN THE RAIN. In this scene they are trying to film a musical number (the year is 1927 and talkies have just arrived) but Lina's voice keeps drifting in and out of the microphone each time she turns her head!

In SINGING IN THE RAIN, Debbie Reynolds meant this pie for Gene Kelly, but he ducked.

And "famous star" Lina Lamont got it right in the kisser.

Gene Nelson and Doris Day in LULLABY OF BROADWAY, 1951.

Ethel Merman is singing "You're Not Sick You're Just in Love" to Donald O'Connor in CALL ME MADAM, 1953.

Joan Crawford had a dubbed-in, operatic singing vo[ice] in TORCH SONG, 1953.

Esther Williams in MILLION DOLLAR MERMAID, 1952.

Judy Garland (right) "doin' the Black Bottom" in A STAR IS BORN, 1954.

One of Marilyn Monroe's most famous numbers was "Diamonds Are a Girls Best Friend" from GENTLEMEN PREFER BLONDES, 1953.

Natalie Wood as Gypsy Rose Lee in GYPSY, 1962.

Barbra Streisand as a pregnant bride-to-be in FUNNY GIRL, 1968.

Sets reminiscent of the 1930's were present in WHAT A WAY TO GO!, 1964, with Shirley MacLaine and Robert Mitchum.

Julie Andrews "vamping down the street" in THOROUGHLY MODERN MILLIE, 1967.

Shirley MacLaine was one of those easy girls to get along with in SWEET CHARITY, 1969.

Ingrid Bergman decided she liked the younger generation's music and danced up a storm in CACTUS FLOWER, 1969.

Even the great Mae West singing "You Gotta Taste The Fruit" in MYRA BRECKINRIDGE, 1970, couldn't save the film.

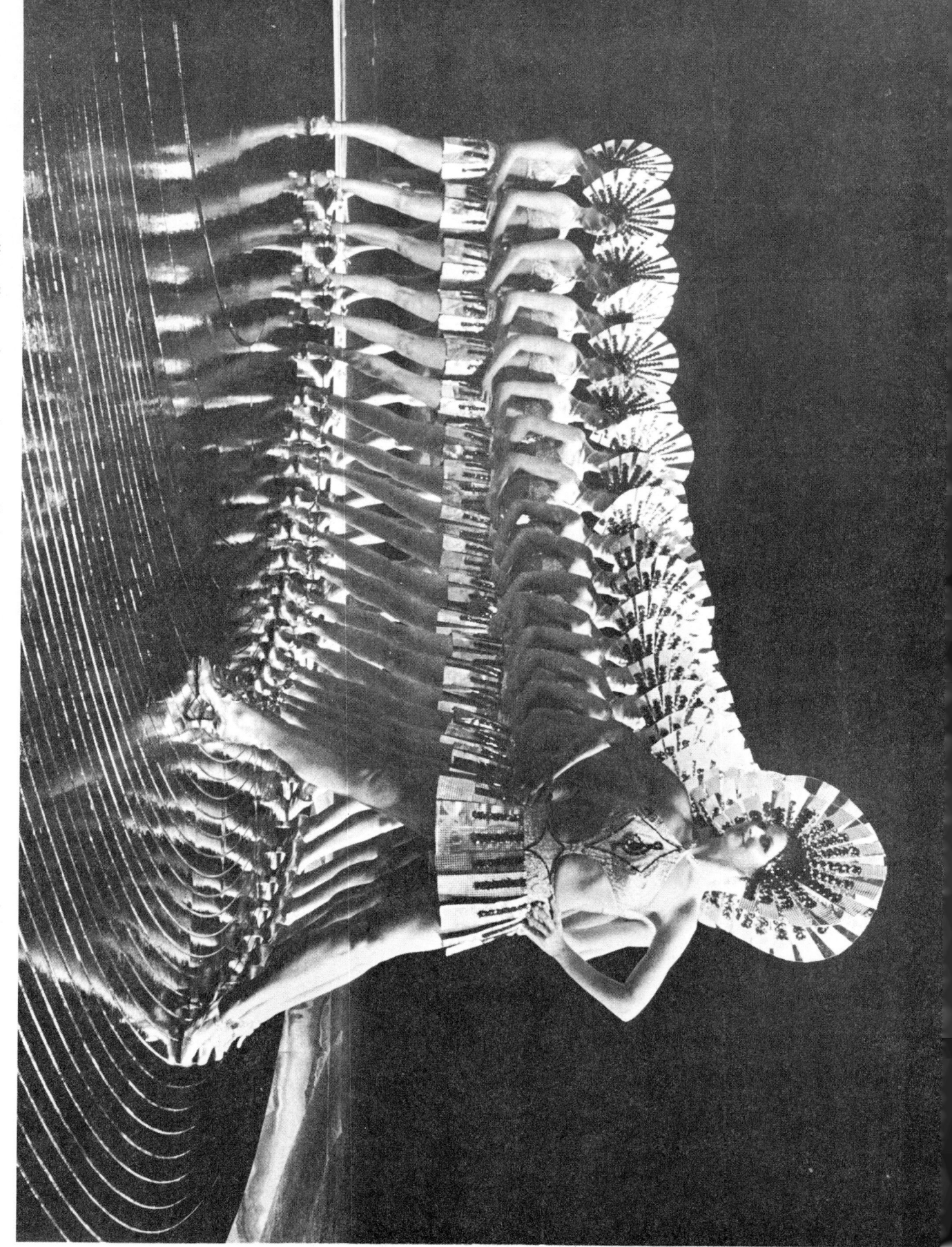

All Hollywood musicals were rolled into one film in Ken Russell's THE BOY FRIEND, 1971.

Liza Minelli dropped coins down her bosom and Joel Grey dropped them down his pants in the "Money, Money" number from CABARET, 1972.

7

SEVEN MOVIE QUEENS

Bette Davis (left) first appeared on the screen in BAD SISTER, 1931. During a visit to "The Steve Allen Show," Steve thought it amazing that in her first film she was already a bad girl. Bette corrected this point by stating she played the good sister while Sidney Fox (right) was the BAD SISTER. Steve replied: "He was?"

Miss Davis was a cigar smoking, morphine-addicted Countess in THE SCAPEGOAT, 1959.

It may be harmful to your health, but Bette could always be found with a cigarette, and her smoking was always included by the many people that have impersonated her. This photo shows her on the set of DEAD RINGER, 1964.

You'd crack-up too if a bent over waiter was blocking the view of your menu. Monty Wooley and Bette Davis on the set of THE MAN WHO CAME TO DINNER, 1941.

Bette Davis and Olivia DeHavilland as sisters in IN THIS OUR LIFE, 1942. Their names in this film were "Stanley" and "Roy."

Bette Davis and Miriam Hopkins in OLD ACQUAINTANCE, 1943.

Nothing compares with Bette Davis' all-time, super-camp film, BEYOND THE FOREST, 1949. She played Rose Moline, a woman married to a small-town doctor (Joseph Cotton) who can't stand her dull life.

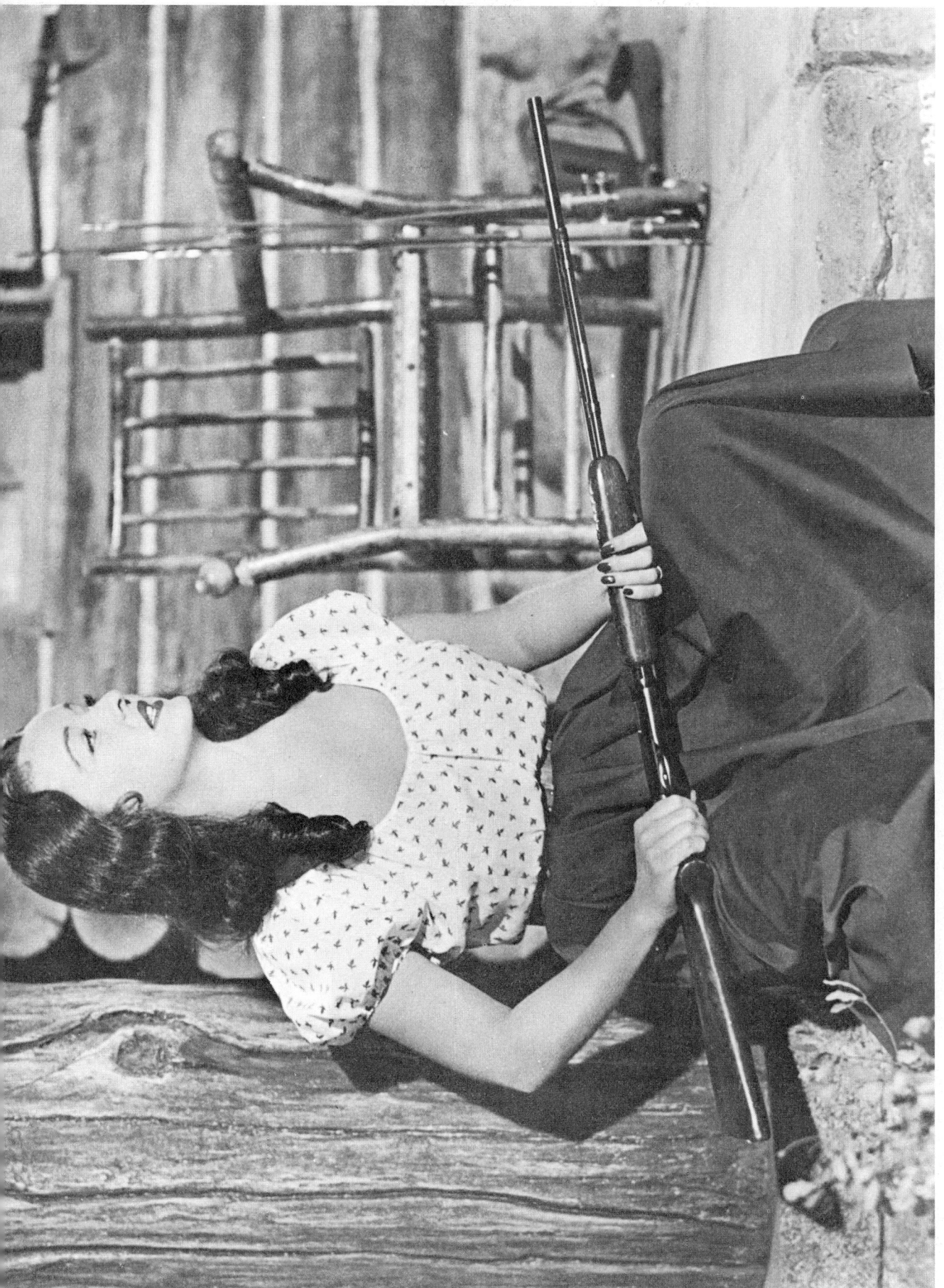

Rosa Moline, just sitting around again, has just shot a porcupine out of a tree. Asked why she did that, Rosa replies: "I hate porkys. They irritate me."

Rosa can't wait until she can collect enough money from her husband's patients to take off for Chicago. She says: "If I don't get out of here, I'll die. If I don't get out of here, I hope I die."
But for the moment she has to settle for a stroll to the small town's post office, to see if her lover has written h
In a reference to BEYOND THE FOREST, Edward Albee in his play "Who's Afraid of Virginia Woolf" has his character Martha ask George, her husband, "What was the name of that God-damn Bette Davis movie the one where she's always trying to get to Chicago?"

Her Indian maid easily upsets Rosa. She threatens to fire her, stating: "You get out of this house. No red Indian is gonna' talk like that to me in my own house." Realizing however that no one will then do the house work, she settles for writing the word "slut" on the dirty table.

She finally gets to Chicago after collecting overdue accounts from the poor patients. Rosa can't get in touch with her lover, so in the meantime she contents herself to talk to room service.

Finding out she's going to have a baby makes her afraid her lover will reject her, so she returns home and jumps down a steep hill to induce a miscarriage. This is a studio publicity shot, and with a fake cliff and backdrop, you can be sure Bette didn't jump too far! In case you're wondering how all this comes out, Rosa gets sick, but determined to make it back to Chicago, she gets dressed, crawls to the train, and dies as it pulls out of the station. And that's the end of BEYOND THE FOREST, 1949.

IE STAR, 1953, Bette played a once-famous actress, Margaret Elliot. Now a een, she gets drunk and lands in jail. Unable to find work, she takes a n a department store, and these ladies, recognizing her, say that a store dn't hire a jailbird. "Take a good look ladies. It *is* Margaret Elliot, waiting couple of old bags like you." One of the ladies replies: "You can't talk to is way, I'll call the manager." Margaret: "Call the manager, call the dent, call the fire department. I won't be here." With that Margaret s out, announcing: "I am Margaret Elliot, and I'm going back to where I emain Margaret Elliot."

In THE ANNIVERSARY, 1968, one of Bette's sons in a transvestite, collecting women's undergarments from clotheslines. When he almost gets caught and comes running home in a sweat, Bette remarks: "You look like you've been trapped in a pantie factory."

A 1928 ad for "The Joan."

Miss Crawford is with Jack Carson in MILDRED PIERCE, 1945.

Constance Bennett, Joan Crawford, and Sally O'Neill
in SALLY, IRENE AND MARY, 1925.

A publicity shot for
HOLLYWOOD CANTEEN, 1944.

This is definitely a publicity still! Joan Crawford and Gibson Gowland, on the set of ROSE MARIE, 1928. On his television show, "Tonight," Johnny Carson asked Miss Crawford exactly what she was supposed to be doing in this publicity still. Joan replied, "You know, I didn't know then, and I don't know now."

Apparently Rex Lease is wondering if the studio couldn't have found a better wig for Joan Crawford in LAW OF THE RANGE, 1928. Joan doesn't appear too happy about it, either.

Do you think Joan was really skating in THE ICE FOLLIES OF 1939? If she wasn't, James Stewart and Lew Ayers were just there "for support."

In 1933 Joan Crawford was obviously not on the Board of Directors of Pepsi-Cola.

With over eighty films to her credit, Miss Crawford appeared in only a few Westerns. Here she is as "Vienna," owner of a gambling saloon, who the townspeople try to bounce out of town in JOHNNY GUITAR, 1954.

Nor was she in 1944!

1942

In publicity stills the *star* gets first chance at facial expression, even if it means that co-star Cliff Robertson doesn't get to emote much. AUTUMN LEAVES, 1956.

It will be up to the reader to decide who has more make-up on, Nils Asther or Joan Crawford in this scene from LETTY LYNTON, 1932.

Martha Raye as "Myrtle Finch" in WAIKIKI WEDDING, 1937. In this scene Myrtle is calling a pet pig who is named Wafford.

Martha's name was "Martha Bellows" in THE BIG BROADCAST OF 1938.

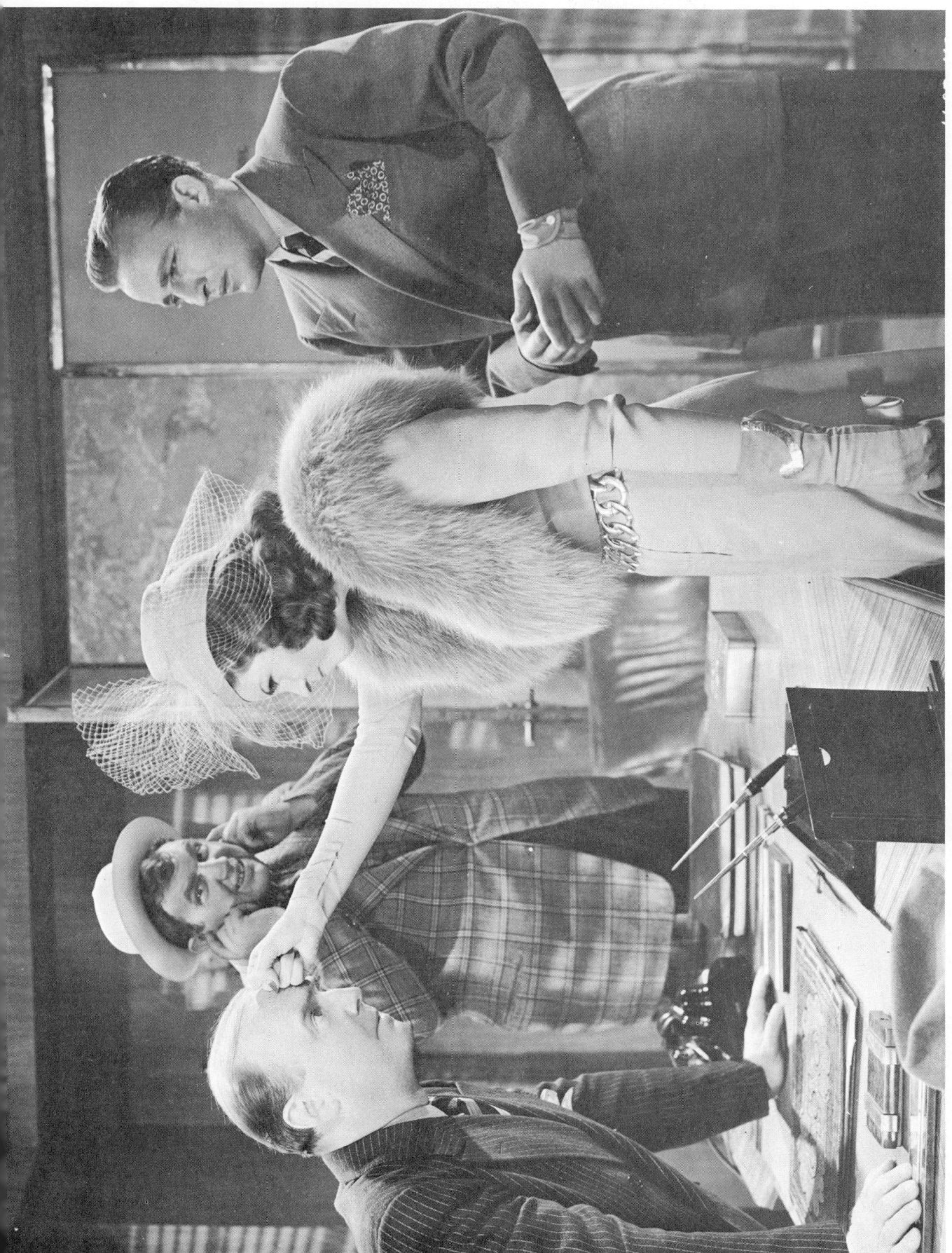

William Frawley, Andy Devine, Martha Raye, and Bing Crosby in DOUBLE OR NOTHING, 1937.

Martha was the Queen of hillbilly swing in MOUNTAIN MUSIC, 1937.

Jack Haley, Martha Raye, Jack Oakie, and Ann Sheridan in NAVY BLUES, 1941, billed in publicity campaigns as the "Miracle Maritime Musical."

Bud Abbott and Martha Raye in KEEP 'EM FLYING, 1941. Martha was often referred to as the "Ultra Violet-Raye."

Joe E. Brown and Martha were in PIN UP GIRL, 1944.

Martha Raye, Kay Francis, and Mitzi Mayfair were Hollywood ladies entertaining at "camps" overseas in FOUR JILLS AND A JEEP, 1944.

Miss Raye as "Annabella," one of the rich wives Charlie Chaplin married with the intent to bump off in MONSIEUR VERDOUX, 1947.

Joan Davis, circa 1937.

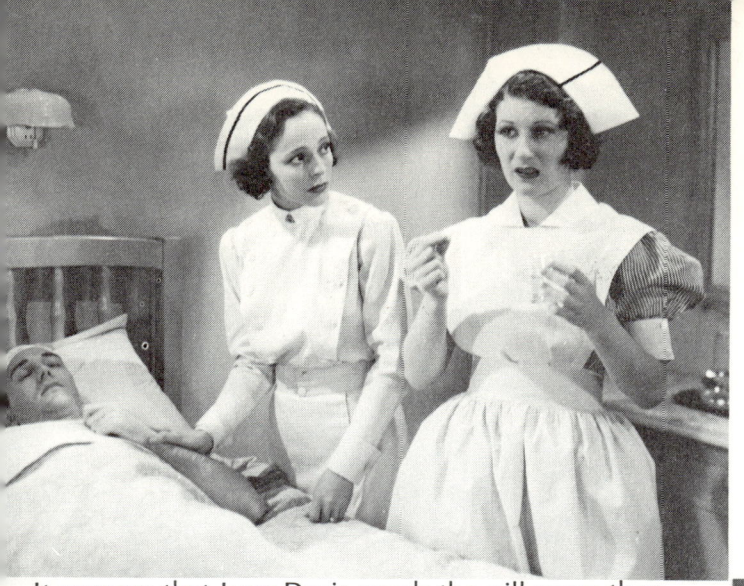

It appears that Joan Davis needs the pill more than the patient. She is with Sally Blane in THE GREAT HOSPITAL MYSTERY, 1937.

Nat Pendleton and Joan Davis in LIFE BEGINS IN COLLEGE, 1937.

...ert Lahr, Joan Davis, and little Shirley Temple in JUST AROUND THE CORNER, 1938.

Miss Davis is TOO BUSY TO WORK, 1939.

Don Beddoe and Joan Davis in
TWO LATINS FROM MANHATTAN, 1941.

Joan was repentant in YOKEL BOY, 1942.

Joan Davis, Eddie Cantor, and Sheldon Leonard in IF YOU KNEW SUSIE, 1947.

Tallulah Bankhead, noted wit and actress, was often referred to as the only woman in America who could be recognized just by her first name. She was also unique for her deep throaty voice. Once Broadway columnist Earl Wilson asked her if she was ever mistaken for a man over the phone. "No," she answered, "Were you?"

In LIFEBOAT, 1944, Miss Bankhead is a newspaperwoman who escapes a torpedoed ship and manages to bring into the LIFEBOAT her camera, mink coat, typewriter, and Cartier bracelet. In this scene Tallulah is discussing the art of tattoos with John Hodiak.

OF A ROYAL SCANDAL, 1945, Tallulah remarked: "I don't know how much history there was in my characterization of Catherine The Great, but I had a lot of fun making it." The story dealt with the private life of the Czarina of Russia, connoisseur of handsome young men, this time William Eythe. In no time at all he became a general in charge of the palace guard.

DIE! DIE! MY DARLING! was the last screen appearance by Miss Bankhead, but after that film was completed, her voice was used for the character of "The Sea Witch" (right) in THE DAYDREAMER, 1966.

Although Mae West was the 1930's reigning "Queen of Sex," this is one of the very few photos in which the Queen displayed her gams.

Miss West's first screen appearance was in 1932, a "test" to see if this well known Broadway star could "make it" in films. The film turned out to be her only appearance in which she did not get top billing.

Not only did she get top billing, but with Mae writing her own screenplays, everyone was at her feet! Owen Moore is the gentleman about to get a diamond in the kisser in SHE DONE HIM WRONG, 1933.

If you look close, there appears to be a white "halo" around Mae's posterior in I'M NO ANGEL, 1933. It's not something Cary Grant caused, but is actually a bad job done by the photo "retouching artist."

Miss West, as a lion-tamer in I'M NO ANGEL, even managed to stick her head in this particular lion's mouth.

Mae West and Randolph Scott in GO WEST, YOUNG MAN, 1936.

Miss West got bounced out of "Little Bend" for carrying on with a masked bandit in MY LITTLE CHICKADEE, 1940. She not only acted with W. C. Fields but co-authored the script with him as well. The advertisement referred to them as a "prairie flower and a nose in bloom."

Mae improved herself and became a school teacher in MY LITTLE CHICKADEE. In less than five minutes she taught boys history, addition, subtraction, and the fact that Cleopatra used to "fool around with snakes."

A slightly exaggerated piece is this 1967 photo-drawing of Miss West, forwarded to members of her still-present fan club.